Proclamation 3

Aids for Interpreting
the Lessons of the Church Year

Pentecost 3

John B. Rogers, Jr.

Elizabeth Achtemeier, series editor

Series B

FORTRESS PRESS   Philadelphia

Library of Congress Cataloging in Publication Data

Main entry under title:
Proclamation 3.

Consists of 28 volumes in 3 series designated A, B, and C which correspond to the cycles of the three year lectionary. Each series contains 8 basic volumes with the following titles: Advent-Christmas, Epiphany, Lent, Holy Week, Easter, Pentecost 1, Pentecost 2, and Pentecost 3.
1. Bible—Homiletical use. 2. Bible—Liturgical lessons, English. I. Achtemeier, Elizabeth Rice, 1926–   .
BS534.5.P765   1985   251   84–18756
ISBN 0–8006–4106–X (Series B, Pentecost 1)

To Anne
with whom Genesis 2:18–24
and Mark 10:6–8 are
grace and life.

Contents

Series Foreword

Proclamation 3 is an entirely new aid for preaching from the three-year ecumenical lectionary. In outward appearance this new series is similar to *Proclamation: Aids for Interpreting the Lessons of the Church Year* and *Proclamation 2*. But *Proclamation 3* has a new content as well as a new purpose.

First, there is only one author for each of the twenty-eight volumes of *Proclamation 3*. This means that each author handles both the exegesis and the exposition of the stated texts, thus eliminating the possibility of disparity between scholarly apprehension and homiletical application of the appointed lessons. While every effort was made in *Proclamation: Aids* and in *Proclamation 2* to avoid such disparity, it tended to creep in occasionally. *Proclamation 3* corrects that tendency.

Second, *Proclamation 3* is directed primarily at homiletical interpretation of the stated lessons. We have again assembled the finest biblical scholars and preachers available to write for the series; now, however, they bring their skills to us not primarily as exegetes, but as interpreters of the Word of God. Exegetical material is still presented—sometimes at length—but, most important, here it is also applied; the texts are interpreted and expounded homiletically for the church and society of our day. In this new series scholars become preachers. They no longer stand back from the biblical text and just discuss it objectively. They engage it—as the Word of God for the worshiping community. The reader therefore will not find here the divisions between "exegesis" and "homiletical interpretation" that were marked off in the two earlier series. In *Proclamation 3* the work of the pulpit is the context and goal of all that is written.

There is still some slight diversity between the several lections and calendars of the various denominations. In an effort to overcome such diversity, the North American Committee on a Common Lectionary issued an experimental "consensus lectionary" *(The Common Lection-*

ary), which is now being tried out in some congregations and which will be further altered at the end of a three-year period. When the final form of that lectionary appears, *Proclamation* will take account of it. In the meantime, *Proclamation 3* deals with those texts that are used by *most* denominations on any given Sunday. It also continues to use the Lutheran numbering of the Sundays "after Pentecost." But Episcopalians and Roman Catholics will find most of their stated propers dealt with under this numbering.

Each author writes on three lessons for each Sunday, but no one method of combining the appointed lessons has been imposed upon the writers. The texts are sometimes treated separately, sometimes together—according to the author's own understanding of the texts' relationships and messages. The authors interpret the appointed texts as these texts have spoken to them.

John B. Rogers, Jr., is minister of the First Presbyterian Church, Shreveport, Louisiana. A graduate of Davidson College and Union Theological Seminary in Virginia, Dr. Rogers taught at Presbyterian College in Clinton, South Carolina, and served two churches in North Carolina before moving to Shreveport. He and his wife, Anne, are the parents of two children.

The Context of Pentecost

At its deepest level, the lectionary is the creation not of a committee or even of the Church, but of one Life. This is clear when one reads through the lessons appointed for the seasons of the sacred year.

There is Advent, with its prophetic word of encouragement and its call to trust in the Lord "who works for those who wait for him."

The prophetic word becomes the Christmas tidings of great joy and deep mystery. But then Epiphany follows, and we ponder just what it means that it is "unto us" that this child is born, and we ask, Who is this?

The meaning begins to deepen as Lent arrives, and Holy Week, with their focus upon suffering and rejection, baring to us the very heart of God who will go to any lengths—to hell and back, if need be—in order to be God with us here in the heart of darkness and the valley of the shadow of death.

Finally, Easter, with the gospel of resurrection: the faithfulness of God who can let himself be nailed to a cross and still not be done for; the promise of God-with-us that cannot be thwarted; the love of God from whom nothing will ever be able to separate us.

Over it all is the mystery of One who, whether or not we can find him or want to find him or care to search, will never let us go, and from whom as from some "Hound of Heaven"—and this is our judgment and our hope—we can never escape.

Yes, from Advent to Easter, it is abundantly clear that one Life dominates the lectionary.

It is the season of Pentecost, then, covering some six months from Pentecost Sunday to the Sunday before Advent, that affords the church a time to reflect upon and to struggle with the life, death, and resurrection of Jesus Christ. The lessons for Pentecost represent the way in which that one Life opens into all the questions and challenges of human existence, and fills with its influence—its indicatives of grace and its imperatives of command—every field of endeavor and duty, until it is worldwide, indeed universal, in its range and significance.

The Sundays in Pentecost included in this volume represent the final movement of the Christian year, gathering to a crescendo. On the twentieth Sunday after Pentecost we see human life and its most intimate relationships not as ends in themselves, but as gifts whereby we are made ready for the grace of God whose very nature is to be God with us and for us, whose name is precisely this promise (cf. Exod. 3:1–15), and who, in the fullness of time, comes to us in one whose name is Emmanuel.

The same point is made on the twenty-first Sunday, this time from the perspective of *our* search for life and for God. Once again, in the story of the rich young man, we are reminded that not only life, but the faith and obedience necessary for authentic living, are gifts of grace—not attainments or accomplishments.

Perhaps the most difficult question of human existence upon which this one dominating Life of the lectionary bears is the question human suffering poses about the nature of God and the meaning of faith. On the twenty-second Sunday the Pentecost lectionary speaks to us of the God who, in Jesus Christ, is with us so completely that he is "touched with the feeling of our infirmities."

The twenty-third, twenty-fourth, and twenty-fifth Sundays after Pentecost face us, in order, with the relationship of grace to faith, to obedience, to stewardship, and place each of these aspects of our "religion" under the searching judgment and matchless mercy of God in Christ.

Finally, the twenty-sixth Sunday and the last Sunday after Pentecost, Christ the King, bring the Christian year to a grand climax with an apocalyptic underscoring of the sovereignty of God to whom belong time, existence, and the whole of creation. Moreover, God's sovereignty is exercised in the rule of grace—the grace of the Lord Jesus Christ, ruler of kings on earth. At the end of the Christian year, when all is said and done, that is a fitting testimony to the significance of Jesus Christ for us and for our world. It is a good word to end on any time, and it also prepares us to embark one week later on yet another Advent journey to Bethlehem and beyond.

The Twentieth Sunday After Pentecost

Lutheran	Roman Catholic	Episcopal	Pres/UCC/Chr	Meth/COCU
Gen. 2:18–24	Gen. 2:18–24	Gen. 2:18–24	Gen. 2:18–24	Gen. 2:18–24
Heb. 2:9–11 (12–18)	Heb. 2:9–11	Heb. 2: (1–8) 9–18	Heb. 2:9–13	Heb. 2:1–18
Mark 10:2–16	Mark 10:2–16 or Mark 10:2–12	Mark 10:2–9	Mark 10:2–16	Mark 10:2–16

When Jesus' opponents tried to engage him in a discussion about "rights" within marriage, he bade them consider God's purpose and will for their whole existence. The Pharisees had asked him, "Is it lawful for a man to divorce his wife?" (Mark 10:2), but it probably was not a serious question. No Pharisee would have had to ask. They knew as well as Jesus did what the law said about divorce (cf. Deuteronomy 24). Their bogus question grew out of an attitude that sought the greatest advantage within the limits of what was permissible—the kind of calculating that destroys a marriage before it begins. At any rate, these Pharisees expected to thrust and parry with Jesus on the surface of life. Suddenly they found themselves plunged into the deeps where the issues are God and humanity, origin and destiny—"From the beginning of creation, 'God made them male and female'" (Mark 10:6).

They sought rights and advantages; Jesus tells them that life is dependent, obligatory. They seemed to want to live under God and with one another by bargains struck and deals made—quid pro quo. They would reduce God and life to a manageable and masterable formula against guilt, fear, and inconvenience. They wanted to talk *permission.* Jesus talked *commandment:* "For this reason a man shall leave his father and mother and be joined to his wife, and the two shall become one" (Mark 10:7). With that commandment he pointed to a gracious will and to an intentional love beyond their wildest imaginings—a grace and love that had held them from the foundation of the world, that had never let them go, and apart from whom they could not hope to get life and relationships right.

Since they knew the content, if not the meaning, of the Torah as well as he did, Jesus took them back to Genesis—to the foundation of the world: "In the beginning . . . God created man in his own image; . . . male and female he created them" (Gen. 1:1a, 27; cf. Mark 10:6). He faced them with the origin and mystery of male and female that is so wondrously described in the story that is the Old Testament lesson.

The story tells of the common origin of man and woman in the will, intention, and creative act of God. The point is not authority, status, rank; the point is *relationship*, intended and structured into human existence by a gracious and loving Creator. When God observes, "It is not good that the man should be alone" (Gen. 2:18), we are given to know that the work of creation is not complete apart from one with whom the man, *'ādām,* can *co-respond*—that is the most complete meaning of the Hebrew *kenegdo,* translated variously "help*meet*" or *"fit* helper."

The story describes God's creation and the man's naming of the creatures of earth and air; but in none of these over whom he has dominion can *'ādām* find his co-respondent. Human sovereignty only points to what is lacking, to what *'ādām* cannot secure for himself, to what only God who made him can provide for him, to what *'ādām* can only receive as he received his own life.

So God creates the woman. It is a divine act. It is not a human accomplishment. It is not a natural occurrence. Just as the Creator formed and breathed life into dust taken from his earth, so from his sleeping *'ādām* he takes a rib and makes woman. The man does not participate in the creation of the woman except as one upon whom God acts. It is all of God, all of grace. "In the image of God . . . male and female he created them" (Gen. 1:27).

Next, like the father of the bride, God brings the woman to the man. The scene suggests neither domination nor submission, only gratitude which erupts in the joyous shout: "This at last is bone of my bones and flesh of my flesh!" (Gen. 2:23b). The wondrous mystery of woman and of her origin in God is obvious to the man, as is the fact that his own existence is now made complete. He is no longer alone. The man and woman are in relationship—co-responding—and that, at last, *is* good.

Good, yes, but perhaps one should not so quickly say "at last." As wondrous and wonderful as a human relationship is in itself, it is not an *end* in itself, either in fact or in this powerful story. Adam may have thought so: "This at last is bone of my bones!" but anyone who has ever been in love will not blame him for getting carried away.

The significance of the relationship of the man to the woman does not end here. Granted, the story goes on to base the historical and human phenomena of marriage and family in the created order as part of the divine intention: "Therefore a man leaves his father and mother and cleaves to his wife, and they become one flesh" (Gen. 2:24). However, we still cannot say "at last." Although the establishment of a home and the becoming one flesh, both in the physical union of man and woman, and in the conception and birth of children, are made fundamental to human existence—even that, accompanied as it is by the wonder of physical intimacy and the absence of shame, does not permit us to say "at last."

Still more wondrous and profound is that in being made for relationship, in being given the capacity to co-respond to and with another, humanity is made ready for *God*. Whatever the story tells us about marriage, about family, about intimacy—and it tells us a great deal about these things—it is even more profoundly a story about human beings made ready for grace, prepared from the foundation of the world for the grace of God. That is, when God graciously elects to come to humanity, he will engage us *in relationship;* he will come personally, indeed, *in person.* Whatever else it might be, the nature of God's involvement with us will be personal—the relationship of an "I" to a "thou." In the capacity for relationship that is part of our human nature and being, we catch sight of God's claim upon us and his intention to be with us and for us as Emmanuel.

The biblical drama confirms this time and again. In the prehistory of Genesis' early chapters, God engages the man and woman as "I" to "thou." "Where are you?" he says to the disobedient Adam and Eve; "What is this that you have done?" Again, "You, Cain, where is your brother, Abel? What have you done?" Even as particular relationships of men and women, husbands and wives, families, tribes, and nations go wrong and break apart on the rocks of pride and selfishness, exploitation and violence—even then God continues with his human creatures, patient in his presence, searching in his judgment, tenacious in his mercy that will not give them up.

In the patriarchal sagas of Abraham and Sarah, Isaac and Rebekah, Jacob and Rachel, Joseph and his brothers, God continues his personal care as Keeper and Provider. The same is true with Moses, and through Moses with an entire people: "I have *seen* the affliction of my people who are in Egypt, and have *heard* their cry . . . I *know* their suffering, and I have *come down* to deliver them . . ." (Exod. 3:7–8).

Even when the people become a nation, with all the grief, intrigue, and tragedy that accompany this, God remains faithful to his promise and intention. To David, he speaks as to a son (2 Sam. 7:12–15a, 16). And so it went across the ages; God engaging his people as Judge and Redeemer, as Savior and Provider.

The prophets of Israel even spoke of the relationship as if it were a marriage. Hosea compares Israel to an adulterous wife running off after other gods as a harlot chases her customers. Deutero-Isaiah uses the marriage metaphor to describe God and his people reconciled (Isa. 54:5–8). In another oracle, Hosea pictures God as a grieving parent suffering over a beloved child gone wrong (Hos. 11:1–9). Over the generations the language of biblical worship and prayer grew rich with metaphors of God's personal involvement with his people: "The Lord is gracious and merciful, slow to anger and abounding in steadfast love" (Ps. 103:8; cf. Exod. 34:6; Jon. 4:2).

That "gospel" persisted, echoing down the centuries, until in the fullness of time the creative Word of God sounded again in the ear of a young woman of Nazareth, and in response to that word there was born One who was called Emmanuel—God with us. Of that one, faith confessed: "The Word became flesh and dwelt among us" (John 1:14); and the author of the Epistle to the Hebrews wrote: "In many and various ways God spoke of old to our fathers by the prophets; but in these last days he as spoken to us by a Son . . ." (Heb. 1:1–2a). Finally, in what is a compelling commentary on Genesis 2 (and a very creative use of Isa. 8:18), this same author wrote: "For he who sanctifies [Christ, our Judge and Redeemer] and those who are sanctified have all one origin. That is why he is not ashamed to call them brethren, saying . . . 'Here am I, and the children God has given me'" (Heb. 2:11, 13).

Now we can say "at last." For in Jesus Christ the purpose of human existence that originated with God "in the beginning" comes clear at last. Here in its most intensely personal form is the grace for which human existence and each and every life have been made ready from the foundation of the world.

The Fourth Gospel tells us: ''He came unto his own'' (John 1:11). And even if ''his own'' will not receive him, as the sad history of humanity over the ages attests, we cannot say that we are not his. From the outset we are his. We are made for him. We have no existence behind us in which we might have been prepared for something other than the grace of God. We have no existence ahead of us in which we might be ordained for something other than God's grace. Individually and in our relationships we are bound up in the life of God: our past, our present being, our future ''hid with Christ in God'' (Col. 3:3).

Now admittedly, we are a long way from where the Pharisees began with Jesus. Jesus, however, had a reason for taking them down to the deeps of life and love; nor was he naive. He knew something about the dynamics of marriage and home and family. He had observed marriage and parenthood in his own home and in the homes of friends and followers. He knew that to take the gift of marriage and reduce it to an abstract legal and social structure was to invite precisely the attitude concealed in the Pharisees' question—the attitude that always wants to know where one can find areas unfettered by legal requirements and that is always asking after rights and advantages, loopholes and edges. From there it is not very far to the pain and chaos of marriage commitments casually regarded and abandoned willy-nilly.

Jesus did know that the human enterprise is sustained by wonder at the mystery of the other; and without this wonder, a relationship almost inevitably degenerates into exploitation. Jesus did know that the human enterprise is sustained by reverence for the intimacy, the knowledge, the unity in marriage whereby two persons are bound in mutual obligation, exclusiveness, responsibility, permanence. Jesus did know that to hear the story of paradise in the midst of our own particular situation, with whatever brokenness in our own life that includes, is to be reminded of another Life and Origin that are ours—another home where, disobedient children though we are, we are not disinherited but are made welcome in the Father's house.

Notice at this point in all the lessons (Gen. 2:18–24, Mark 10:13–16, and the quotation from Isa. 8:18 in Heb. 2:13) how the references to the birth and nurture of children are linked to God as the one who gives and undergirds life. In his answer to the Pharisees, Jesus surely knew that our marriages and family lives are never more than a poor reflection of God's intention. But in the human mystery of marriage and parenthood, broken though it may be, we are given a metaphor for the grace and love and life of God by which alone we live. Indeed, this grace and love and life that surround us "as the air" form the context in which we may deal with our human relatedness and brokenness, as persons and as families, with honesty, with confession, with compassion.

Jesus seems to be saying that the metaphors of home—marriage, family, parenthood—still have much to commend them. This is not true because our concept of the family or our handling of the gifts of marriage and parenthood are adequate to God; it is true because family experiences involve us in relationships through which the reality of God-in-Christ can shine, both to point to him and to redeem the meaning of the family for us. Time and again the Old Testament speaks of God's parental presence and care. Jesus also spoke often of God's fatherhood and home. He prayed: "Our Father . . ." (Matt. 6:9); "Father, into thy hands I commit my spirit!" (Luke 23:46). He illustrated life in the kingdom of God by a little child. He described the sovereign grace of God in terms of a father's love drawing a prodigal son back from the far country and welcoming him home. That Jesus chose marriage, parenthood, and home as symbols of God's being toward us and of our being made for God is itself a clue to the meaning of life.

That is why, when the Pharisees questioned him, Jesus took them to the heart of God and let them see what somehow they had missed; namely, that they and their relationships had their origin in God, were linked to God, and were rooted in his grace. Martin Luther called Jesus "the mirror of the Fatherly heart of God." Long before Luther, the author of Hebrews had the same thing in mind when he wrote: "For He who sanctifies and those who are sanctified have all one origin. That is why he is not ashamed to call them brothers [and sisters], saying, 'Here am I, and the children God has given me'" (Heb. 2:11, 13).

It is as if, in Jesus Christ, God comes to us in person, sweeps our shallowness aside, claims us as his own possession, takes even our brokenness upon himself and into his heart, and throws his everlasting arms around our life and death with a shout: "Here at last is bone of my bones, and flesh of my flesh!"

The Twenty-first Sunday After Pentecost

Lutheran	Roman Catholic	Episcopal	Pres/UCC/Chr	Meth/COCU
Amos 5:6–7, 10–15	Wisd. 7:7–11	Amos 5:6–7, 10–15	Prov. 3:13–18	Amos 5:6–7, 10–15 or Wisd. 7:7–11
Heb. 3:1–6	Heb. 4:12–13	Heb. 3:1–6	Heb. 4:12–16	Heb. 3:1–6
Mark 10:17–27 (28–30)	Mark 10:17–30 or Mark 10:17–27	Mark 10:17–27 (28–31)	Mark 10:17–27	Mark 10:17–31

"Seek the Lord, and live!" (Amos 5:6a). Eight centuries earlier that had been the urgent word of the prophet Amos to a nation on the brink of catastrophe. Life is linked to God, Amos had reminded them: in its origin, in its conduct, in its destiny. "Seek the Lord, and live!" There "seek" means not simply to inquire about God or to look for God, but to turn to God and hold to God, as it were, for dear life. It is as if Mark had Amos's word in mind as he crafted this account of Jesus and the rich man into his Gospel.

As is Mark's style, the scene begins abruptly: "And as Jesus was setting out on his journey, a man ran up and knelt before him and asked him, 'Good Teacher, what must I do to inherit eternal life?'" (Mark 10:17). That Mark tells us he knelt is not incidental (cf. Matt. 19:16; Luke 18:18); it is a subtle but conscious suggestion that God and life are linked not merely in principle, but also in person. "Seek the Lord, and live!"

There is in this dramatic scene, from the outset, an awareness that life is under an ultimate sovereignty. Life is not "of itself," but given; it is not accidental, but structured in grace and held in steadfast love; it is not autonomous, but responsible. The point is made in virtually every line of the story. The man kneels to Jesus. Jesus points to God. The Ten Commandments place life itself and each life in particular, including the rich man's life, within the domain and under the sovereign will of God. If you and I understand the Ten Commandments only as a guide for the life over which we ourselves remain master and judge, we have not understood enough. Symbolized in the Decalogue and made flesh in Jesus Christ, the command of God claims a man or woman for God.

"You know the commandments," said Jesus. The "Ten Words" were the quintessential linking of God and life. They represent the just and compassionate ordering of life, growing out of reverence for God and worship of God as Lord of life, and issuing in righteousness and reverence for the life of the neighbor (cf. Mic. 6:8).

"Teacher, all these things I have observed from my youth" (Mark 10:20). The note of despair is still in the man's voice, and apparently he is still on his knees. And yes, there is something wrong with what he says, though not what we usually suspect. His words are testimony to a devout life. This is not self-righteous boasting. While self-righteousness is always a danger for a man like this, that is not the problem here. Even if he proves to be a hypocrite, making himself out a saint when, in fact, he has broken every commandment, Jesus does not seem to be interested. The man does not strut arrogantly up to Jesus. His response does not betray a smug self-satisfaction: "Ah, the commandments. Yes, I'm glad you mentioned them. I've done very well by them, if I do say so." He runs up and falls on his knees; and there he remains in anguish: "Teacher, all these things I have observed from my youth." What must I do yet? What more? Whatever I have done, it is obviously not enough, else why this anxiety and emptiness that will not let me rest? Give me something more to do! Give me another commandment that I can take into the sphere of my own sovereign will and obey. Give me some ethic to master, some goal to reach, some sacrifice to make, so that I can put my life in order to get it right!

Do we begin to understand the problem now? This man has allowed the command of God to determine his action; he is willing to continue doing so. He even throws himself before Jesus and asks, "What must I do?" But he remains his own master, his own judge, his own lord. His problem is a problem we all have, but it is especially a problem for successful people—people who, through their skill, competence, and self-discipline, have learned that life can frequently be made to respond to them. This man who comes to Jesus is like any good, successful, righteous man or woman who, when asked what is the most important thing in life, will answer without hesitation, "My relationship to God"; but who never once realizes that he or she treats even this "most important thing" as something that is his or hers to establish, to cultivate, to maintain. "If what I have done is not enough, as apparently it is not, that is O.K.," the rich man seems to say, "What more must I do; just tell me; I'll do anything. But I will do it in the free decision and by the determined action of my own sovereign will."

Now before we too quickly add our deprecating nod to this exposure of "Pelagianism," look at the next line in the story. "Jesus looking upon him loved him . . . " (Mark 10:21a). It sounds almost like an offhand comment, and one is wont to hurry over it in order to get to the command that proves to be the man's undoing. But do not be in such a hurry. "Jesus, looking upon him, loved him." That is the operative word in the whole drama of the rich man, casting its light into every dark corner.

"Jesus looking upon him loved him." In the man's seriousness and zeal for the things of God, in his self-discipline and determination, in his burning devotion (at least by standards he chose to use), Jesus loved him. Even when it all proved to be an admirable and noble form of disobedience that had left him restless and empty and unsatisfied, Jesus loved him. Jesus declared himself *for* this man—he really loved him and never stopped loving him.

"You lack one thing; go, sell what you have, and give to the poor, and you will have treasure in heaven; and come, follow me" (Mark 10:21b). It is only here that we learn of the man's great wealth. Perhaps it was his successful mastery and management of his possessions that misled him about who's who and what's what in the kingdom of God. At any rate, this man who, according to Mark, knelt to Jesus now hears from this same Jesus the command of God that is both his judgment and his hope.

"Go, sell what you have [or rather, what you do not have at all but what has you] and give to the poor. . . . " The more afraid we are that this command means literally what it says, the more we probably need to hear it precisely that way. John Calvin said that the rich were actually "God's ministers to the poor," and he spoke of the poor being sent to the rich—to people like those of us who read and use this book, and those in the congregations we serve—as God's test of our stewardship. According to the Gospel, suggested Calvin, theft is not only the act of grabbing something that belongs to another; theft is first of all refusing to give to our neighbor that which love ought to give.[1] "Go, sell what you have, and give to the poor. . . ." Again, compassion, generosity, reverence for life are inalterably present where life is linked to God.

Then, "Come, follow me." Mark would have us see in the man's kneeling to Jesus what the man himself did not even see, namely, that in Jesus Christ we encounter the One for whom we are made, to whom we belong, and apart from whom there is neither life nor satisfying work nor rest. In Jesus Christ, Mark seems to be saying, competence is driven to its knees and given the gift of true humility—the gift of knowing that we come from Another, that we belong in every moment to Another, and that we are destined for Another.

"At that saying his countenance fell, and he went away sorrowful; for he had great possessions" (Mark 10:22). Shattered by the command of God that confronts him in what Jesus says and in who Jesus is, the man went away sorrowful. He is unmasked and seen at last to be disobedient. For him the command of God sounded as judgment, and he went away sorrowful. The last we see of him, he is still in bondage to what he has and to what he is in and of himself.

Commenting on the judgment of God, Karl Barth wrote: "The most terrible thing that God can do to us [is] simply to let us proceed."[2] This means, from our point of view, that we arrive at our personal goal—the top rung of that economic, social, political ladder we have been climbing, the pinnacle of that professional, vocational, academic, religious summit we have been striving to reach—and God is not there. It means that we become what we want to be, achieve what we want to achieve, without God. That is the most terrible hell: when our planning succeeds, our goal is reached, and God is not there—not there along our way, not there amid our striving, and most certainly not there at our end. That is our downfall—the judgment within the grace of God.

We are not told what happened to the rich man. He does not show up again in the biblical drama. What we do know—and this is the *grace* within the *judgment* of God—is that the man is not abandoned by Jesus Christ. "Jesus looking upon him loved him." That word still stands. The man is still loved; and he still lives, disobedient and sorrowful though he is, in the kingdom of Christ. He cannot withdraw from the kingdom of Christ—from the rule of grace. It includes even the disobedient in their misery. He cannot get away from the fact that Jesus loves him. Moreover, the command of God: "Go, sell . . . give . . . follow me" will always be near him even as he goes away sorrowful. Still he is held in grace and, therefore, is not without hope. You and I may never forget that "Jesus looking upon him loved him."

As Karl Barth has suggested, Jesus Christ does not will to be without the rich man; he wills to be with him and for him. For whom else is Jesus there but for the disobedient? Whom else has God loved from eternity? The rich man can reject what Jesus commands. He can go away, as he did do. But he cannot get outside the boundaries of the kingdom of Jesus Christ. He cannot throw off or escape the rule of grace. He cannot destroy the inalienable and decisive fact that Jesus loves him—loves him, the obdurate and evasive rebel who returns to the darkness without any of the Gospels having any reason to tell us what became of him. That Jesus loves him is the only thing we can cling to in his favor quite apart from what he does or does not do. But can we cling to anything better in our own or any one else's favor?[3] As with the disciples we watch the rich man go away sorrowful, we are reminded of James Russell Lowell's lines:

. . . behind the dim unknown,
Standeth God within the shadow
Keeping watch above His own.
(James Russell Lowell, "Once to Every Man and Nation")

We may find it easy enough to see ourselves in the rich man. However, in case we do not or cannot or will not take our stand with him, Mark continues: "And Jesus looked around and said to his disciples, 'How hard it will be for those who have riches to enter the kingdom of God!' and the disciples were amazed at his words" (Mark 10:23–24a). Their amazement here is the same as at other times in Mark's Gospel when God-in-Christ breaks through to human consciousness and understanding: for example, when a demon is cast out—who but God had that power? (cf. Mark 1:27); or, when he healed the paralytic with the words, "My son, your sins are forgiven"—who but God could forgive sin? (cf. Mark 2:12); or, when he rebuked the wind and the sea—whose but God's voice had nature ever obeyed? (cf. Mark 4:41). Now again, they were amazed. They had seen a man offered life—who but God can do that? And the man went away sorrowful.

As the disciples watch the rich man go away, and as Jesus speaks directly to them, it is as if suddenly it begins to dawn on them that they are with Jesus and belong to him. Here they are: a fishing boat abandoned and a tax desk and who knows what else, to follow him. And this is the amazing thing: They are here, they begin to realize, not through any sovereign decision of their own. They are here because in Jesus Christ something, or rather someone, had taken hold of them, and they had no real choice but to be where they were.

He continued: "Children, how hard it is to enter the kingdom of God! It is easier for a camel to go through the eye of a needle . . . " (Mark 10:24b–25a). The disciples quickly realize their solidarity with the rich man. They realize that the command of God—the offer of life: "Go, sell . . . give . . . come, follow me"—runs counter to every person's anxious concern about himself or herself, about possessions and status, and about one's relationship to God (there it is again, that "relationship to God" that we are so concerned to control). Even those who are obedient, like the disciples, are always on the edge of disobedience. And they are astounded because, even as obedient disciples, they know their solidarity with the rich man.

Only so does their next question make sense: "Who then can be saved?" (Mark 10:26b). Their question places all men and women—all of us who establish our own security by what we have and what we do and what we are—in the same predicament as the rich man. Indeed, if it is true that life, salvation, faith, obedience are finally within our competence, and if it is true that the origin and conduct and destiny of life are under the control of your sovereign will and mine, then we are in trouble. For according to this story, given the choice, we won't make it—can't make it, really, since what we like to call "free will" is really self-will that so controls us that we are free neither for God nor for neighbor. There is as much chance that we will put right our lives and our life together as there is that a camel will go through a needle's eye, an utter impossibility.

The disciples knew this and asked, "Who then can be saved?" to which Jesus replied, "With men it is impossible, but not with God; for all things are possible with God" (Mark 10:27). Life and salvation, faith and obedience are finally in the gracious and omni-competent hands of God. For all our searching for God, the truth is that we are graciously sought and found by God himself who, in Jesus Christ, gives us life and calls us and sets us free for service in his name. We are not left to do the impossible. By the grace of God, we are participants in the impossible possibility. As the disciples watch the rich man go away sorrowful and as Jesus' words fall on their ears, they are given to know, in no uncertain terms, the astonishing truth we toss off so frequently as a euphemism: "There, [literally] but for the grace of God, go I."

Reinhold Niebuhr knew something about life under the judgment and grace of the impossible possibility. His words sound as wisdom for our living.

> Nothing that is worth doing can be achieved in our lifetime; therefore we must be saved by hope. Nothing which is true or beautiful or good makes complete sense in any immediate context of history; therefore we must be saved by faith. Nothing we do, however virtuous, can be accomplished alone; therefore we are saved by love. No virtuous act is quite as virtuous from the standpoint of our friend or foe as it is from our standpoint. Therefore we must be saved by the final form of love which is forgiveness.[4]

The command of God that addresses us in Jesus Christ is both a threat and a promise. It threatens every pretension whereby we hold on to life and seek to have God on our own terms. It is at the same time a persistent promise that pursues us to hell and back, whatever form our disobedience may take. We should take heart that in this command, God stakes his claim upon our lives. It is under that claim that we live, together with the disciples and with the rich man, to our judgment and to our eternal hope.

The contribution of the Epistle lesson (Heb. 3:1–6) to the sermon which moves from Amos to the Gospel story of the rich man is of the nature of a descant underscoring the general theme of our participation in what God has done in Jesus Christ. No longer is it a matter of what I must do, but of being graciously set free to respond to God's command not because we *must,* but because we *may*—indeed, because we can do aught else but live in the kingdom and under the rule of God's sovereign grace in Jesus Christ, with all the impossible possibilities that involves.

The Twenty-second Sunday After Pentecost

Lutheran	Roman Catholic	Episcopal	Pres/UCC/Chr	Meth/COCU
Isa. 53:10–12	Isa. 53:10–11	Isa. 53:4–12	Isa. 53:10–12	Isa. 53:4–12
Heb. 4:9–16	Heb. 4:14–16	Heb. 4:12–16	Heb. 5:1–10	Heb. 4:9–16
Mark 10:35–45	Mark 10:35–45 or Mark 10:42–45	Mark 10:35–45	Mark 10:35–45	Mark 10:35–45

The Old Testament and Epistle lessons remind us that biblical faith is not a philosophy built up from below. It is a response to the weight and presence of a Life beyond our own from whom and through whom and to whom are all things.

From the opening curtain of the biblical drama to its grand finale, this Someone is present, sometimes front and center, sometimes mysteriously hidden, but always effective. The drama begins with the mysterious and majestic word that calls the world and life into existence. It must be a musical drama, by the way, because the Book of Job tells us that on that day "the morning stars sang together, and all the children of God shouted for joy" (Job 38:7). The whole business ends with the Hallelujah Chorus—at least, Handel took his text from the Revelation: "Hallelujah! For the Lord God omnipotent reigneth. . . . The kingdom of the world has become the kingdom of our Lord and of his Christ, and he shall reign forever and ever!" (Rev. 19:6; 11:15). The one decisive fact and redeeming presence in the whole of it is just God himself.

The Epistle lesson with its powerful imagery is very much to the point: "For the word God speaks is living and active, sharper than any two-edged sword. . . . And before him no creature is hidden, but all are open and laid bare to the eyes of him with whom we have to do" (Heb. 4:12–13). The Word of God is not some announcement of truths about God; it is God himself. Mark that—it is not the human race or human history that stands at the center of things. It is not armed forces or noble ideas; it is not world politics or commerce or the Bible or religion. God is at the center. Human life revolves around God: in its triumph and tragedy, its hope and fear, its grandeur and failure, its insight and ignorance, its reverence and arrogance. The nations revolve around God, and the years as well.

The Word of God is not an argument for God. The Bible never seeks to prove God from the logic of time, nature, or being. God moves in on us from the pages of the Bible in the mystery of his being and his nature, his will and his purpose, piercing like a sword to the very center of our being where mind and heart, will and strength are knit together.

If we come to the Bible looking for anything else, we ask it for what it cannot give—for answers it does not have and has never had. The Word of God is not a scheme for knowing future details and the timetable for the end of the world. The Word of God is not God's declaration of whose side he is on in war; it is not some ideological blueprint for a new social order or a divine sanction for the present one. The Word of God is not a mere historical record calculated to send us off on quests for Noah's ark. No, in the Bible there comes a word: "I will be with you"; "I will be there for you"; "I am . . . " (cf. Exod. 3:12, 14) the wisdom and the will, the grace and the power, the purpose and the compassion, the truth and the life back of all created things. It is God's offer of himself. We do not have to take it; we can deny it or ignore it or scorn it. But the word God speaks is "living and active, sharper than any two-edged sword, piercing to the division of soul and spirit, of joints and marrow, and discerning the thoughts and intentions of the heart. And before him no creature is hidden, but all are open and laid bare to the eyes of him with whom we have to do."

We put so much stock in what we think of God or in what we decide about God—sometimes it is called "evangelism"—when the important thing is what God thinks of us and what he has long since decided about us. The Bible contains a word that exposes us to God. It lays us open to his grace and to his judgment and to the urgency and invincibility of his purpose. It wraps us in the circle of his presence and power. It is the place where, alone and in our life together, we are "laid bare before the eyes of him with whom we have to do."

According to Hebrews, that is not a very comforting prospect. Who among us could bear the holiness and righteousness of that look? Who could survive it? The very thought of it drove the young Martin Luther to the monastery and very nearly out of his mind. In another place, the author of Hebrews says: "It is a fearful thing to fall into the hands of the living God" (Heb. 10:31). What would be worse, however, would be to fall out of the hands of God altogether. There is, after all, a worse fate even than the judgment of God; and that is if God should cease to judge us, should withdraw himself, and cut us adrift. The worst thing that could come to us is the conviction that what we do does not really matter because we do not matter, even to God.

When we put our minds to it, it is a little surprising that we still do matter to God. Presumably, as the biblical story unfolds, God could have canceled the whole business at any time, having had every provocation. Of course, that is projecting our impatience and exasperation onto one whose thoughts are not our thoughts, nor our ways his ways (cf. Isa. 55:8). Our tendency to do this is rooted in an understanding of power that rules by intimidation and coercion and that, when thwarted, resorts to vindictiveness, giving up and lashing out for want of a better way. It is the approach to things that, on the human level, leads to domestic violence and to physical and emotional abuse in families. It is the approach to things that leads to violent crime, and to a system of criminal justice that is more concerned with vengeance than with safety—a vicious circle of violence that brutalizes a society. It is the approach to things that, on the international level, leads to oppressive governments, violent revolutions, terrorism, invasion, war, and that brings the world to the brink of self-destruction.

According to the biblical story, when God saw what kind of world he had to deal with, he said in effect: "Very well. You refuse to trust me and to obey; I shall not force you. I shall not use my power to coerce or intimidate. I shall face your power with my grace. I shall stand in front of your little pharaohs and fuhrers, your Pilates and Caesars. I shall endure your denials and betrayals. I shall merge with your hungry and thirsty, your nameless strangers and your naked poor, your sick and your prisoners. I shall bear your brutalities and mount your gallows and suffer your holocausts. And we shall see!"

As the drama unfolds, we do see the God who will not let go or give up. It is there in Psalm 103, at the heart of biblical worship, where life is responsive to the weight and pressure of God's presence (Ps. 103:8–12). It is in the Book of Exodus where, early on, the covenant is broken and the commandments have to be rewritten (Exod. 34:4–7). It is there centuries later, as the pouting Jonah argues with this God who, he knows to his dismay, cares even for the Ninevites (cf. Jon. 4:2). Over and again that note is sounded: "Gracious, merciful, slow to anger, abounding in steadfast love." Of course, this could be simply a projection of human wishes into the void—a kind of cheap grace. But what if it is the response of human life laid bare to the eyes of him "with whom we have to do"? Then it would not be cheap grace at all, but the steadfastness of love, the persistence of mercy in, with, and beyond the judgment that pierces like a sword and lays life bare to the holy and righteous gaze of God.

Notice how this grace takes shape in the story. At one point, on the pages of the Old Testament, in the writing of the prophet we know only as Deutero-Isaiah, a mysterious figure appears who is called the "servant of the Lord." Our Old Testament lesson is a portion of the last and longest of four songs of the prophet about this strange figure. At first God speaks, proclaiming the servant's achievement and exaltation which, he says, will astonish kings and nations because they are confronted with a completely unexpected vindication of the humiliated servant. A group speaking in the first person, presumably representatives of the nations, next recounts the change that has come over them through the servant. They had seen no reason in his birth, his person, or his life to think him significant; he was unlikely, unattractive, and unwanted. But now they know that the very suffering which made them avoid and despise him was his way of taking their sin onto himself and bearing their guilt and punishment for them. Somehow, they say, God willed this to be; and this servant quietly did his Lord's bidding. He suffered in submissive silence, was put to death in obscurity, and buried in shame. But now they confess that it was all the plan of God to reclaim them for himself. In opaque yet specific terms, they speak of an existence of the servant beyond his suffering in which his vocation for himself and others is brought to completion, and God's purpose fulfilled. At the conclusion, God speaks again to declare that the Servant will be honored as one who has won a victory over the powers of sin, death, and evil in the world.

The figure is not named, yet his portrayal as an individual is so detailed as to approach biography. He listens to God. He submits to God's vocation. He is not just a witness, but brings salvation in his own person and career. He is given no identity; and therein lies the great mystery of this passage. When the Ethiopian eunuch encounters Philip, the deacon (Acts 8), he is reading this passage from the prophet. "About whom, pray, does the prophet say this," the eunuch asks, "about himself, or someone else?" Whose is this role? There is only one way to know. Someone must be found—or must find us—of whom, when we see him, we can say: "He poured out his soul to death, and was numbered with the transgressors; . . . he bore the sin of many . . . " (Isa. 53:12). Indeed, someone must be found of whom we are compelled to say: "Surely he has borne our griefs and carried our sorrows; . . . he was wounded for our transgressions, he was bruised for our iniquities; upon him was the chastisement that made us whole, and with his stripes we are healed. All we like sheep have gone astray; we have turned everyone to his own way; and the Lord has laid on him the iniquity of us all" (Isa. 53:4–6). Has such a one come to us?

Albert Outler recently suggested that the Epistle to the Hebrews is really less an epistle than it is a fifth gospel—a gospel placed strategically in the New Testament canon, after the Pauline letters with their emphasis on the divine nature of Christ, to give a balancing emphasis upon Christ's humanity. After a full dose of Paul, we have to take Hebrews for the side effects and understand that not only in Jesus Christ do we have to do with God himself, but also in Jesus Christ God graciously elects to be intimately involved with us in our humanity. He takes our humanity upon himself—not our perfect, flawless, healthy, blameless, triumphant humanity, but our humanity with all its pain and guilt, its brokenness and despair. He takes our lives—even takes our dying—upon himself so that he is, in the marvelous words of the King James Version of the text, "touched with the feeling of our infirmities." The Creator—Judge— Redeemer of the universe who swings the stars in their courses and guides the destinies of nations is "touched with the feeling of our infirmities."

If this is the one with whom we have to do, before whose eyes we are laid bare, then whatever radical surgery his word may perform at the depths of our hearts and minds and lives, his word is not finally brandished as a weapon but is an instrument of healing. Whatever judgment we may be dealt by his hand, that hand is not finally put forth to destroy, but to save.

In many and various ways God spoke of old to our fathers by the prophets; but in these last days he has spoken to us by a Son . . . He reflects the glory of God and bears the very stamp of his nature . . . (Heb. 1:1–3a).

Since then we have a great high priest . . . Jesus, the Son of God, let us hold fast our confession. For we have . . . a high priest who is . . . touched with the feeling of our infirmities, . . . one who in every respect has been tested as we are, yet without sinning. Let us then with confidence draw near to the throne of grace, that we may receive mercy and find grace to help in time of need (Heb. 4:14–16).

We suggested to begin with that the Old Testament and Epistle lessons remind us where the life of faith begins: not with us, not with some shining ethic, not with some noble cause, not with some healthy projection of human benevolence onto the cosmos. It begins above us and beyond us—with God. The life of faith began long ago: a Word that commanded the universe to be with laughter and singing; an exodus from Egypt; a birth in Bethlehem; a cry of God-forsakenness from a lonely hillside; a death on a cross; a resurrection, quivering with mystery—all simply to illumine the deepest mystery of all. It is the mystery of the love of Almighty God for human beings—all of them and each of them. It is the mystery of a God who loves so much and cares so much for our life that he has chosen to be "touched with the feeling of our infirmities"— our sickness of body and mind and spirit, our fear of death and of life, our guilt, our self-destructiveness, our unbelief, our loneliness—"touched with the feeling of our infirmities."

No doubt we are laid open and laid bare before the holy, righteous, penetrating eyes of him with whom we have to do. No doubt it is a fearful thing to fall into the hands of God. But in Jesus Christ we are given to know that the one with whom we have to do and into whose hands we fall is, for all that, "touched with the feeling of our infirmities."

One thing more needs saying. This life of faith that God begins thus is not a life of ease. Our Epistle lesson from Hebrews contains a word about a "Sabbath rest" for the people of God, but the reference harkens back to the completeness and fullness of God's creation—the purposefulness and right working of what God has made—not a kind of nonchalant, self-indulgent carelessness in the name of faith. We are not invited to withdraw into a snug harbor and leave God's world to God and call that Christian faith.

The Gospel lesson, Mark 10:35–45, with its emphasis on servanthood, insures that we do not snuggle up with our faith as a private security blanket. But notice how Jesus gets at the servant concept in that passage. *Diakonos* means one who belongs to another, and it stands in direct contrast to one who, as a "ruler" *(archon)* or as one of the "big shots" *(megaloi)* lords it over another. It is a theologically loaded word, and it has as much to do with our relationship to God as with our relationship to the world. This is especially important in shaping our understanding of mission. It reminds us whose witnesses we are and whose commission we hold. It is a word which, if its full meaning is heeded, may help us to avoid confusing our own agenda with God's agenda, or reinterpreting God's causes to match our own (whether of the left, right, or center) under the noble guise of "service," "praxis," "evangelism," or "justice"—all ideologically defined.

The faith to which the Word of God calls us is neither an indulgence, nor a substitute for obedient living, nor a technique for getting around difficulties, nor an invitation to make the world (or the church) conform to our agenda in God's name. "The god who is primarily a helper toward the attainment of human wishes is not the one to which Christ said, 'Thy will, not mine, be done.'"[5] There may be no less pain for us because we believe, no less care, no less privation, no less distress. That God is "touched with the feeling of our infirmities" does not mean that we shall be given a detour around adversity. It is not a promise to soften the hard realities of existence. It is a promise that when we go through the deep waters of life, we shall not do so alone. It is the promise that in the struggle for justice and peace and righteousness in our world, in every dark night of the soul, in the valley of every shadow (even the shadow of death), even if we descend into hell, we are accompanied and held fast by God who is with us, not as a stranger, but who is himself "touched with the feeling of our infirmities."

The Twenty-third Sunday After Pentecost

Lutheran	Roman Catholic	Episcopal	Pres/UCC/Chr	Meth/COCU
Jer. 31:7–9	Jer. 31:7–9	Isa. 59:(1–4)–19	Jer. 31:7–9	Jer. 31:7–9
Heb. 5:1–10	Heb. 5:1–6	Heb. 5:12—6:1, 9–12	Heb. 5:1–6	Heb. 5:1–10
Mark 10:46–52	Mark 10:46–52	Mark 10:46–52	Mark 10:46–52	Mark 10:46–52

The Old Testament lesson comes from that part of the prophecy of Jeremiah known as "The Book of Consolation" (chaps. 30—31). A mixture of poetry and prose, these collected prophecies of hope are a moving testimony to the divine grace from a prophet whose message, for the most part, was one of judgment against the religious apostasy, moral decay, and ethical carelessness of the people of Judah. The judgment with which Jeremiah had threatened his countrymen through the years was never simply the vengeance of God. It was the discipline of God. In principle at least, it could be averted by sincere repentance. Failing that, it was the discipline of God whose purpose was the reconciliation and healing of his people—not their destruction. Thus, even as Judah persisted in her unfaithfulness and apostasy and as the judgment of God hastened toward her undoing, Jeremiah could point beyond judgment to the future of God's people—to a time of healing and hope (Jer. 31:8–9).

This is the constant theme of the Book of Consolation. In another part (Jer. 31:20), God speaks as a brokenhearted parent, tortured and torn between the punishment and forgiveness of a wayward child. There are echoes here of a similarly moving poem in Hos. 11:1–9. Again, in words that constitute one of the truly great passages in all of prophetic literature (and that are especially appropriate to mention if the Eucharist is being celebrated in the service), God speaks through the prophet of a future of reconciliation and restoration, God and humanity bound heart to heart (Jer. 31:31–34). Through the whole of the biblical drama runs this tension between human existence, broken and beyond all hope of healing save by the mercy of God, and the gracious promise and persistence of this God of mercy who will not quit until what is broken is made whole again. "Behold, I will . . . gather them from the farthest parts of the earth, among them the blind and the lame . . . " (Jer. 31:8).

Now with that promise as a kind of overture, we come in Mark's Gospel to the story of blind Bartimaeus. There is, no pun intended, more to the story than meets the eye. It will take some sharpening of our vision to see the full picture.

For one thing, we need to remember how the miracle stories function in the Gospels. On the way from Jericho to Jerusalem, Jesus comes to the place where a blind man begs beside the road. Read quickly through the Gospel of Mark and notice how many times something like this occurs—Jesus confronted and interrupted in the course of his ministry by some form of human suffering.

In 1:14–15, Mark gets to Jesus' ministry right away, after a word about John the Baptist and a brief account of his baptism of Jesus and Jesus' temptation in the wilderness. It is striking how soon and how often thereafter Mark shows Jesus confronting this "whatever it is" that binds and burdens and blinds and breaks human beings, in mind and body, in heart and health, in life and in hope—how often and in how many different forms: demons, disease, disability, death, and even nature's devastation in the form of storms at sea. And every time, there is a word or a touch that lifts the burden, releases the captive, reclaims the outcast, forgives the sinner, calms the fear, and restores life to wholeness and peace. Mark's point seems to be that in this Jesus of Nazareth, in what he says, in what he does, in who he is, there are an authority and a power that belong to God alone.

Mark may not have begun his Gospel with a Christmas story. He may not, with Matthew, identify Jesus as Emmanuel—God with us. He may not, with Luke, bring Jesus on stage with a herald angel announcing, "Unto you is born . . . a Savior . . . " and a chorus singing the "Gloria in excelsis." There is in Mark no echo of John's *mysterium tremendum:* "And the word became flesh and dwelt among us. . . . " But from the beginning and over and over, this earliest and shortest of the Gospels is punctuated with the sense of awe and wonder with which Mark would touch us and with the questions he would have us face and wrestle with and answer for ourselves (cf. Mark 1:27; 2:12; 4:41; 5:42; 6:51; 7:37). This is Mark's way of proclaiming that in Jesus of Nazareth—in his overcoming the power of evil, in his authority to forgive sin, in his power to make human life whole and human again, in his word that even the wind and the sea obey, we have to do with God himself, with us and for us, in person. But Mark makes this proposal in such a way that his readers are aligned with the crowds, the disciples, and the questioners: "Who then is this?" What say ye?

In his classic monograph, *The Meaning of Revelation,* H. Richard Niebuhr wrote: "Revelation means for us that part of our . . . history which illumines the rest of it."[6] Revelation is that event from which we can go forward or backward, and so attain some understanding of the whole. "That event to which we appeal in the Christian church is . . . Jesus Christ in whom we see the righteousness of God. . . . Revelation means God, God who discloses himself to us through our history as our Knower, our Author, our Judge, and our only Saviour."[7]

Just so, the miracle stories of the Gospels are the testimony of faith. They are told not so much to create faith as to testify in faith, and often in retrospect, to the mysterious power of God in this Jesus about whom they were told. They do not offer easy answers or neat explanations. Instead, and especially in the way Mark employs them, they purposely leave us shaking our heads and asking: "Who then is this?" A good and righteous man? A prophet of God? A heroic and compassionate carpenter? A wise rabbi? A visionary dreamer? Or is this one in whom the power and purpose, the presence and person of God himself take hold of us in awesome judgment and redeeming mercy, in steadfast love and amazing grace?

For another thing, we need to notice how this particular miracle story is employed by Mark and crafted into his Gospel. The story of Bartimaeus is the second of two incidents in the Gospel of Mark in which a blind man receives his sight. The first occurs just before the midpoint of the Gospel. It concludes the first phase of Jesus' ministry as Mark presents it, in which the primary emphasis has been on Jesus' mighty deeds. As we saw, in his early chapters Mark has sought to underscore the power and authority of this one who casts out demons, heals the sick, forgives sin, raises the dead, rules the forces of nature, and puts the most broken and outcast of human lives back together.

What begins to dawn on us as we read along is that, according to Mark, the disciples apparently did not understand! Of all people, these

twelve of the inner circle seem not to have been able to answer the
question raised by the person and activity of Jesus. Just before the first
incident with a blind man, Mark lets us in on Jesus' perplexity over their
"hardness of heart" and their failure to understand. Right on the heels of
the miracle of the feeding of the four thousand, the disciples are worried
about having nothing to eat. In Mark 8:17–18, 21, we can almost hear the
exasperation in Jesus' voice. Has it all been to no avail?

Six verses later we come to the famous "watershed" in the Gospel of
Mark—Peter's confession on the road to Caesarea Philippi—the first
acknowledgment of Jesus to be the Christ of God. The bridge between
blindness and insight, the doorway that leads from confusion to confession, is a miracle in which a blind man is given his sight. In the structure
of his Gospel, Mark makes strategic use of this story to say: Unless God
opens our eyes—unless God gives sight to the eyes and insight to the
minds and light to life—then even those who appear to be closest and
claim to understand most are, in their perception of the kingdom of God,
as blind men. This is Mark's dramatization of Paul's statement in Ro-
mans that "there is no distinction; since all have sinned and fall short of
the glory of God, they are justified by his grace as a gift . . . " (Rom.
3:22b–24).

Like this first account of a blind man, the story of Bartimaeus stands,
not accidentally but strategically, at the end of the second phase of Jesus'
ministry. After Peter's confession, the emphasis in the Gospel of Mark
shifts somewhat, as if a turning point has been reached. From that point
on, Jesus' face is set toward Jerusalem and the cross. We hear less about
Jesus' mighty works and more about his teaching, which focuses on the
cost of discipleship and the suffering and death that loom on the horizon.

As for the twelve disciples, it is as if they had suffered a relapse into
blindness! Three times in three chapters (8:31; 9:31; 10:32–34), Mark
tells us that as they went along, Jesus spoke very frankly to them about
where their way would lead. Each time the disciples missed the point
completely! In 8:31–33, Peter argues with Jesus, and is harshly rebuked:
"Get behind me, Satan!" In 9:33–34, the disciples fall into an argument
about who is the greatest. In 10:35–36, James and John ask for status and
power in the kingdom of God. Each time, Jesus counters with a discourse
on the nature of discipleship (cf. 8:34ff; 9:35ff; 10:42–45).

With that, Jesus sets out with the disciples on the last leg of his journey

to Jerusalem. On the way he comes to Bartimaeus.[8] Like the way to faith
and confession, the way to discipleship, the way to obedience and servanthood, is entered only through the eye-opening grace of God. The
first time blind eyes were opened, the disciples found themselves on the
road to Caesarea Philippi. They were carried, by the grace of God, from
blindness to belief, from confusion to confession: "Thou are the Christ!"

Once again, their eyes must be opened. Once again light must come
from beyond them to illumine their minds and lives and to lead them on
the way. Having had their eyes opened to faith and confession, they now
need another ophthalmological miracle to open their eyes to the cost of
discipleship—the cost to God in Christ and the cost to any who will
follow after him. If God must open our eyes to faith before we can even
utter the words of confession, so also must God open our eyes before we
can see to follow Christ into Jerusalem, and into Gethsemane, and to
Golgotha.

Incidentally, the weight of New Testament scholarship regarding the
authorship of the Gospel of Mark is that it was written from Rome and
that it represents the testimony of Peter, either directly under a
pseudonym or more likely related orally to Mark for use in the early
church. If this is true, then Peter is confessing to his readers that for the
longest time he and the others did not or could not or would not understand, that they kept drawing the wrong conclusions about the kingdom
and the Christ, and that finally it was only by the grace of God that their
eyes were opened and their feet set on the right track. It is as if Peter is
confessing: "As close as we were to the action, we did not come close to
understanding! We were blind; we tried to make him conform to our
hopes and plans; we argued about rank and status and power; we betrayed him; we denied him; at the end, we forsook him and fled. Like
blind men we groped in our particular darkness of faith and life until God
opened our eyes!"

What the miracle stories of the Gospels do as a whole, and what Mark
does with particular brilliance in this story of Bartimaeus, is to place us
before the mystery of God-in-Christ. Bartimaeus was, doubtless, a historical figure, the son of Timaeus; and as such his story, in and of itself, is
full of grace and light. But even more, Bartimaeus is for Mark a represen-
tative figure. In the drama of the gospel of God—in the drama of the
dawning of God's kingdom as the sovereign rule of grace—Bartimaeus

was a kind of Everyman. His brokenness, his desperation, his cry for mercy is that of the world, the human family, the human heart, each and every heart after its own fashion. His blindness is our blindness, and that of Peter and James and John, there being "no distinction."

Describing Jesus as the doorway to faith and life, and as a pathway to God, Augustine wrote: "If he had not graciously consented to be the way, we should all have gone astray. . . . I do not say to thee, seek the way. The way itself is come to thee: arise and walk."[9]

Surely, that is the "gospel" that comes through the Epistle to the Hebrews with its emphasis upon and rich metaphors about Jesus' human priesthood. He is the one through whom God himself comes to us, and the one also through whom we come to God. Bartimaeus surely heard this good news in the words of his friends: "Take heart, rise, he is calling you" (Mark 10:49).

"And Jesus said to Bartimaeus, 'Go your way; your faith has made you well.' And immediately he received his sight and followed him on the way" (Mark 10:52). That way led them to Jerusalem, where, on the night in which he was betrayed, as he sat at table with disciples, Jesus took bread and blessed it and broke it and said, "This is my body, broken for you. . . . " As, with men and women across the ages and around our world, we come to his table, does that ancient promise from Jeremiah not still sound its overture to our broken world? "Behold, I will . . . gather them from the farthest parts of the earth, among them the blind and the lame. . . . "

The Twenty-fourth Sunday After Pentecost

Lutheran	Roman Catholic	Episcopal	Pres/UCC/Chr	Meth/COCU
Deut. 6:1–9	Deut. 6:2–6	Deut. 6:1–9	Deut. 6:1–9	Deut. 6:1–9
Heb. 7:23–28	Heb. 7:23–28	Heb. 7:23–28	Heb. 7:23–28	Heb. 7:23–28
Mark 12:28–34 (35–37)	Mark 12:28b–34	Mark 12:28–34	Mark 12:28–34	Mark 12:28–34

"Which commandment is the first of all?" It was a favorite question among the rabbis and scribes, the teachers of Israel. Do certain of the commandments sum up the others? In which ones are contained the heart of religion? Which commandments plumb the deeps of faith and life? One rabbi said that Moses gave 613 commandments: 365 negative and 248 positive. The Ten Commandments epitomize the law given to Moses on Mount Sinai, given into the life of Israel from the hand of God. The prophet Micah reduced the commandments to three (Mic. 6:8); Amos reduced them to two (Amos 5:14–15). Deuteronomy's bequest to the worship of Israel is one great commandment; it is actually the first of the Ten Commandments stated positively (Deut. 6:4).

Rabbi Hillel is reported to have summed up the law for a gentile inquirer: "What you would not have done to yourself do not do to your neighbor: that is Torah, and all the rest is commentary." Rabbi Akiba said that "thou shalt love thy neighbor as thyself" was the great principle of the law. Jesus answered from Deuteronomy and Leviticus (Mark 12:29–31; cf. Deut. 6:4 and Lev. 19:18), and it is the only time in the Gospels where a teacher of the law agrees with him: "And the scribe said to him, 'You are right, Teacher . . .'" (Mark 12:32).

Both Jesus and this unnamed teacher of Israel were aware of the move that is on in Scripture from the world of origin and destiny, the world of purpose and possibility and promise, toward and into the world of human story, the world of human being and deciding and acting. Both acknowledged the transcendent claim upon human life that calls for a response— the pressure upon human existence and upon each and every life of One from whom and through whom and to whom are all things. Jesus says that this movement from the beyond into the midst of human life is nothing less than the sovereign rule of grace—the invincible love of God who, in his reconciling power, redeeming purpose, liberating promise takes hold of us, claims us as his own possession, and gives us to one another for life together. Indeed, where grace does its reconciling and redeeming work in human life and among human beings, there one is "not far from the kingdom."

The point is made here not only by what Jesus says regarding the commandments, but also by the fact that it is Jesus who says it. It is typical of Mark to focus upon Jesus himself as the one in whom the kingdom is at hand—just so close. Here also one begins to hear the descant of Heb. 7:23–28 above the major movement between the Old Testament lesson in Deuteronomy and Jesus' word on the commandments.

Several things are worth noting about Jesus' answer. First, there is the *wisdom* of it. The wise man or woman sees beneath the surface into the depths of things, sees beyond what is obvious to what is significant, beyond what is factual to what is crucial, beyond what is known to what is true. The wise man or woman is not satisfied with knowledge alone, but seeks understanding in a spirit of reverence before the deeper mystery at the heart of life.

One does not have to disdain learning and scholarship, much less make a virtue of ignorance, to recognize that the best informed person is not necessarily the wisest. This is especially important in the face of the "information explosion" that marks our modern world. There is a real danger that in a highly technical, highly specialized society, facts can be and will be used to isolate life from its source and destiny—a danger that in the vast sea of data and information that surges around us, we shall be tempted to ask only about facts and not about truth. Facts can be cornered; data can be catalogued and programmed; information can be classified and codified. Not so with truth. Truth is more than facts and data and information; truth has a transcendent dimension to it—an eternal character rooted deep in the heart of reality, or, one confesses, deep in the heart of God.

In the encounter between Jesus and the scribe, the *knowledge* of a well-informed man is clarified and completed by the *truth* that comes from God. Here the expert, the specialist, the master technician of the law is given a larger vision of origin and destiny, of point and purpose, of the promise and providence that pulse through life like the very heartbeat of God.

Surely that is wisdom for our age as well. This does not mean that religion should rule over science, education, or politics. It does mean that the mystery of life's meaning and purpose is neither solved nor contained within these limits. It means that a theological perspective upon life is not extraneous or anachronistic but essential to wisdom and to wholeness of vision. It means that when questions arise that bear upon the fact and future of human existence—the development, testing, and deployment of nuclear weapons, the pursuit of world peace, the ecological care of the earth, the just and compassionate handling of human life—it is folly to treat them finally as scientific or political questions and to ignore their human and theological dimensions. It is even greater folly to leave their answering to those who have the facts, but who lack the larger vision that sees and knows with the top of the mind and the bottom of the heart that life belongs to Another.

At any rate, in his encounter with Jesus, the scribe learns that human knowledge, however extensive and thorough, needs the grace of greater wisdom, and that the beginning and goal of wisdom is: "You shall love the Lord your God with all your heart, and with all your soul, and with all your mind, and with all your strength . . . and you shall love your neighbor as yourself."

Another thing about the answer Jesus gives is its *depth*. "To have a God," wrote Martin Luther, "properly means to have something in which the heart trusts completely. . . . To have God, you see, does not mean to lay hands upon Him, or to put Him in a purse, or shut Him up in a chest. We lay hold of Him when our heart embraces Him and clings to Him. To cling to Him with our heart is nothing else than to entrust ourselves to Him completely . . . " (Luther, *The Larger Catechism*).

The question comes: What is it that you and I love with our whole heart and mind and will and strength? What is it that I think most about, or worry over most, or work at hardest? What would my wife say? What would my children say? What would my best friends say? What would anyone say who looked deeply into my life?

What is it for us: the great society? Reaganomics? profits? capital gains? religion? personal salvation? the Church? If so, on any of these, to what end? For the comfort and security they promise? Can they really deliver on such a promise? Is our goal a high standard of living, so called? If so, *high* in what worthy sense? and whose is the *standard?* and *living* to what purpose?

Human beings are made to love and to worship, Luther seems to have been saying. Our life is not a shallow pond with no outlet; it is a river flowing deep and to the sea. If we choose to live as if there were no God, we become locked within ourselves and stagnate. If, on the other hand, we create gods in our own image, to serve our own ends, and to sanction our own aspirations, we empty ourselves into a shallow puddle fed only by our selfishness, and so are doomed to dry out in cynicism and despair. There is a command in the very depths of our nature, in heart and soul and mind and will, that will not let us rest. In Jesus Christ, the deeps of origin and destiny in that mystery we call God call to the deeps in us, and something, or rather, Someone draws us to himself. "The Lord our God, the Lord is one; and you shall love the Lord your God with all your heart . . . soul . . . mind . . . strength . . . and you shall love your neighbor as yourself."

Still another thing about the answer Jesus gave is its *breadth.* "You shall love your neighbor as yourself." This God who made us for himself and whom we are commanded to love is always on the move toward us—always loving and judging and forgiving his way into our lives. There are no effective barriers against his invincible grace and his steadfast love. Moreover, he breaks down the barriers all along the spectrum of human life, barriers we erect around and between the human lives that are covered by his love. The familiar hymn declares, "There's a wideness in God's mercy, like the wideness of the sea." To love God is to be drawn into the circle of his love, which embraces the whole of his creation and every creature. This is why Jesus allowed no fences to be built around the word "neighbor." No unworthiness, no repulsion, no racial or national heritage, no barriers of class or culture, no difference of politics or ideology or religion can make a human being other than a child of God and, therefore, a neighbor.

In Luke's Gospel, Jesus' teaching on the great commandment leads into the parable of the Good Samaritan, the story prompted by the scribe asking, "Who is my neighbor?" The inescapable implication of the parable is that a neighbor is anyone who can pull a battered, broken, dying man out of a ditch and save his life—even the most despised outcast one can imagine (which is what the Samaritan represented to Jesus' hearers). If we really want to understand this parable in all its force, we have to put ourselves in the place of the wounded man and, in the place of the good Samaritan, the person or the kind of person we most detest and fear. Whose face would you and I have to be willing to see from that ditch in order to understand the parable aright, and who might cast us in the role of the Samaritan?

We have to do here with a powerful love that will go to any lengths—to the mat, to the wall, to the cross, to hell and back—in order to restore what is broken and reconcile what is separated. So often we soften the impossibility of the thing with the comment: "Oh, we are supposed to love everyone, but we don't have to *like* them." That may be true. It is also trite, especially when we focus on the last part of it and go on holding our grudges, nursing our resentments, and hurling our bitter words and thoughts at life like poison arrows.

The love of neighbor Jesus is talking about is the love that draws its compulsion and strength from God's own love for us across all barriers. This kind of love ought to carry a church's community ministry beyond mere financial aid to personal involvement because those being served and those doing the serving are children of God, neighbors in his redeemed world and brothers and sisters of one Father. It drives us beyond the transient and trivial "Have a nice day" in our hopes and wishes for others, for human beings in need are not creatures of an hour or a day; they have eternal worth. Immanuel Kant said that true neighborliness means treating every person not as a means but as an end. Yet no one can be an end in himself or herself, for each of us is a creature whose origin and end is God. The love of neighbor to which we are called stands against the background of what God has done for us in Jesus Christ and can never be exempt from any needful ministry. The world that shapes the life and heart and mind and soul of any and every neighbor, from the greatest to the least of them, wherever they rank in our estimation—that world itself must be shaped with justice and tenderness, compassion and peace. That is what it means to love our neighbor.

Still another thing about Jesus' answer is that it is *comprehensive.* Note the emphasis on "all" in Jesus' summary of the law. In Matthew's version, Jesus says, "This is all the law and the prophets"—the whole of faith and life, of God's purpose and promise. In Luke's version, Jesus says to the scribe, "Do this and you will live"—live in the fullest and most complete sense of the word. This is life, eternal, from God and through God and to God. Here in Mark's version, when the scribe agrees, Jesus says: "You are not far from the kingdom of God"—not far from the sovereign, invincible rule of grace that leaves no creature outside the love of God and no creature exempt from his command.

Here Jesus reaches to the heights and the depths of existence and to the widest ends of earth and time. "There is no faith without ethics," Jesus' answer says to us, "and no ethics without faith."

There is no faith without ethics. Love of God without compassion for people, without a commitment to justice, without a relentless striving for peace and reconciliation and healing in a broken world or community or family or church is a Christian impossibility. Only one who fears social change or loves security more than he or she loves or fears God can claim that such concern is secondary, extraneous, or secular.

But neither can we have ethics without faith. The sovereign grace and gracious sovereignty of God are the very context in which human life, both personal and corporate, is established, judged, reconciled, and redeemed. This means that part of our Christian vocation is to watch for and listen for the judgment of God as it is brought to bear upon every personal and social issue which threatens to undo the sovereignty of God, the sanctity of human personality, and the responsibility of the human self—so long as we remember that the judging word is God's Word and not ours, and that we ourselves and our causes and priorities are convicted by it as well.

And yet, we need to remember also that because we always stand somewhere between Christmas and Easter, the Word of God to the world, and therefore the church's word to the world, is primarily and ultimately a positive word of grace and love. For it is throughout a word about Emmanuel—God with us—in life and death and destiny. To make the gospel primarily and fundamentally a condemnation, to open up the abyss between God and humanity which the life, death, and resurrection of Jesus Christ closed forever, is not the church's task. The Christian to whom this word of grace is not absolutely the most important word, both personally and vocationally—who first of all wants to shout at, bewilder, scorn, harass, condemn, pressure, manipulate people on account of their perceived ignorance and unbelief, their folly and selfishness—had better remain silent altogether. Peter Taylor Forsyth, the Scottish theologian, wrote: "The world can only be converted (claimed for the gospel) by a Church which believes that in Christ the world has already been won."[10]

This brings us, in conclusion, to the interpretive key to the whole incident, namely, Jesus Christ himself. All along through his Gospel, Mark has brought the question of the presence and power and purpose of God's rule—the kingdom of God, he calls it—to focus in the person of Jesus. God knows, Mark seems to be saying, that men and women do not finally give themselves over to an argument or even to a commandment, but only to a person. We know that we belong not to "thus!" but to a "thou!" Confronted by a proposition or a command, we want to answer or question or quibble or clarify. When the kingdom of God is near, when the rule of grace overshadows us and claims us as subjects, when we stand before God in Christ, we can only be silent. "And when Jesus saw that he answered wisely, he said to him 'You are not far from the kingdom of God.' And after that no one dared to ask him any questions" (Mark 12:34).

The time to question and argue and dispute, says Mark, is over now. It is time to be silent—time to respond in reverent silence and surrender to God's decision about us and God's action for us in Jesus Christ. That is finally our only choice. It is the love of God for us in Jesus Christ that makes possible our even hearing, not to mention obeying, the great commandment. "We love because he first loved us" (1 John 4:19).

The secret to the command of God is the one who speaks it. For in him we encounter the One by whom and for whom we were created, to whom we belong with heart and strength and mind, who is "above all and through all and in all," whose will is our freedom and our peace, whose purpose is our identity and our destiny, and meeting whom along our way as the Word made flesh is at once our judgment and our eternal hope. As Mark here brings Jesus' ministry to a close, he reaches back into the eternal wisdom of God's Word, written, and places the great commandment in the mouth of the Word made flesh.

Over this scene sounds the descant of the Epistle lesson. In Jesus Christ God's love is shed abroad, and in the power of that Love we are able to love God and one another. Indeed, to be "in Christ," as Hebrews declares we are, is also to be "not far from the kingdom."

The Twenty-fifth Sunday After Pentecost

Lutheran	Roman Catholic	Episcopal	Pres/UCC/Chr	Meth/COCU
1 Kings 17:8–16	1 Kings 17:10–16	1 Kings 17:8–16	1 Kings 17:8–16	1 Kings 17:8–16
Heb. 9:24–28	Heb. 9:24–28	Heb. 9:24–28	Heb. 9:24–28	Heb. 9:24–28
Mark 12:41–44	Mark 12:38–44 or Mark 12:41–44	Mark 12:38–44	Mark 12:38–44	Mark 12:38–44

In the Old Testament and Gospel lessons, we meet two widows whose stories remind us that, both in fact and in faith, we live beyond our means. Since the twenty-fifth Sunday after Pentecost so often falls within the annual stewardship/Thanksgiving season in many churches, one might well be on the lookout in these texts for themes appropriate both to the liturgical year and to the congregational life of a particular church. Whether it is "budget time" or not, Thanksgiving is just around the corner, and any celebration of Thanksgiving without a consideration of stewardship is a kind of blasphemy.

First, there is the story of Elijah and the Sidonian widow. "Like a meteor" (Loehr) the strange and mysterious figure of Elijah appears suddenly on the horizon of the biblical narrative, in the middle of the ninth century B.C., in the reign of King Ahab. With Elijah's appearance, there occurs an upheaval in the biblical drama, the dawn of the age of the prophets.

For the narrator/historian of the Book of Kings, Ahab personifies the apostasy of Israel gone to seed—the nation's turning away from the worship and service of God to embrace the fertility gods of Canaan, and the subsequent moral and social disintegration that followed in the wake of that infidelity. Epitomized in Ahab's marriage to the Phoenician princess, Jezebel, the corruption of king and country is sounded in the foreword to the narrative of Ahab's reign (1 Kings 16:31, 33).

With Elijah's arrival on the scene, a strange new theme begins to sound (with growing persistence) in the life of the people of God. Actually, it is not new at all; it is a very old word, but it had become a barely audible whisper in the life of Israel. It is the theme of the sovereignty and grace, the command and judgment, the righteousness and redemption of the Lord God as the controlling reality both in the life of the nation and the life of each individual. It is struck anew by the prophets who, for three centuries, strode across the length and breadth of Israel and Judah to bring the ancient Word of God to bear upon the life of the people, proclaiming to king and commoner in court and countryside: "This is what God has said!" about faith and about life, about worship and about relationships, about justice and about truth, about righteousness and about peace. And at the beginning of this "age of the prophets" stands Elijah. He is not the first prophetic figure we meet, but he stands effectively at the head of the line that runs through Amos and Hosea, Isaiah and Micah, Jeremiah and Ezekiel to and beyond the prophets of the exile.

The stories about Elijah are fraught with the miraculous and the unusual, but through them all runs the theme of the sufficiency and providence of God who is the source of life. We hear it in the very first sentence of the Elijah story, in the first word he utters to King Ahab (1 Kings 17:1). Elijah seems to be saying: "You, Ahab, and Jezebel, and your lot think Baal sends life-giving rain. We shall see who commands the rain, and whose word gives and sustains life!"

The point is emphatically underscored: Elijah is sent into the wilderness where he is sustained by ravens who feed him at the command of the Creator. Then, as an even more emphatic illustration, the prophet is sent *outside* the kingdom of Israel to the area of Sidon. The reader is meant to understand that this is the realm of the Phoenician god, Baal. Here in the encounter with the widow, both the prophet and the woman are given to know that even where Baal is worshiped and regarded as the provider and sustainer of life, it is the Lord God who gives life and who provides bread to sustain it—it is God from whom life derives and to whom it belongs as his own possession. One can almost hear in the background of these stories of God's sustaining providence the words of Ps. 104:27–28.

The one overriding point of the story, the theme that runs through the Elijah cycle like a golden thread, is that life is given and carried, preserved and kept in the gracious providence of God. In the deepest sense of the word, we all live, like Elijah and the widow of Zarephath, beyond our means.

The second story comes from the passion narrative in Mark. It is the story of the poor widow's offering, or the widow's mite as it is popularly known; and it serves as a kind of link between Jesus' public ministry and his passion.

As Mark brings Jesus' ministry to a close in his Gospel, he does so by means of several incidents that focus on the question of faith and that define faith in terms of ownership and stewardship.

Notice how these issues are raised in the twelfth chapter of Mark. First question: Who owns the earth? The parable of the vineyard, with which the chapter begins, makes it clear that "The earth is the Lord's and the fullness thereof, the world and those who dwell therein" (Ps. 24:1). When the stewards of the Lord's vineyard cease to be stewards; when they presume to seize control of what belongs to Another; when the produce of the vineyard is hoarded in careless disregard for the welfare of others whom the owner would feed; when our relationship to the earth is marked not by stewardship but by selfishness, not by gratitude but by greed, not by humility before God's lavish goodness but by hostility to God, to his word, and to his presence, the end is not power but pathos, not dominion but destruction. Who owns the earth? "The earth is the Lord's. . . ."

Second question: To whom belongs the realm of human affairs, of politics and economics? "Is it lawful to pay taxes to Caesar?" By the way, Jesus never really answered that question. He simply used this as an opportunity to raise the more fundamental question of the sovereignty of God in human affairs. His statement, "Render to Caesar the things that are Caesar's and to God the things that are God's," leaves the Pharisees and Herodians and us to consider what happens to the sovereignty of Caesar in relation to the sovereignty of God before whom "the nations are like a drop from a bucket, and . . . the rulers of the earth as nothing" (Isa. 40:15, 23).

We have still to figure this out; we have still to come to terms with the subordination and accountability of Caesar and Caesar's kingdom to the kingdom of the Lord and of his Christ. We continue to place the image of Caesar on our coins and currency; then we add, "In God we trust," with more emotion than understanding of what that might really mean for the undoing and redoing of our national life, and for the undoing and redoing of our priorities and values as a nation under this or any other administration.

Next question: Who owns time? Who rules history? The Sadducees' question about the resurrection betrays their assumption that time is defined in relation to our lives and in terms of the relationships that comprise our particular history. Jesus' answer turns everything around. Time, he says in effect, belongs to God, along with life and relationships. When we think otherwise, when we seek the meaning of time and history in ourselves, we are "quite wrong." Time belongs to the same One who owns eternity. Our lives and our relationships and our history are in his keeping. Rejoice in that. Be confident that for time and eternity our lives, and the lives of those we love, and all that gives focus and shape, meaning and purpose and identity to our existence—all, in the words of the old prayer, that "ministers to our best life"—all this has been and is and will be ordered and brought to completion by one who "keeps your going out and your coming in from this time forth and forever more" (Ps. 121:8).

Then this: Who owns my ultimate allegiance? Who commands my heart and soul and mind and strength? Whose is the command that directs my life and my relationships? The question of the commandments is not really a question about which of them is first or greatest. It is the question about whose commandments they are—whose command it is that we hear and obey. The question is: To whom does my life belong—my life, and the lives I touch with my own? Jesus' summary of the law makes that abundantly clear.

Next there is that strange passage about the relationship of the Messiah to David. It is again a question of ownership. To whom does the Christ belong? Does Christ belong to some culture, to some nation, or to some religious tradition? No. Christ belongs to God, and therefore he belongs to the world across the boundaries of tradition, nationality, culture, and even religion.

So we come at last to the story of the poor widow. Again, the issue is ownership, and now it has come all the way home: Who owns us? To whom do we belong, not just on the inside, not just with heart and soul and mind and strength, but to whom do we belong with all the things that we cling to and that cling to us: wealth, possessions, abilities, expectations, our plans for the future, the goals we set, relationships that come and go? To whom do we belong, as it were, lock, stock, and barrel? It is a scene in which lives, not gifts, are in the balance; and the eyes that are looking on are eyes that nothing can escape.

With this dramatic scene, Mark pushes the question of faith, the question of ownership and stewardship, to its deepest level. Is life, is faith, finally within our means, or do we live, in fact and in faith, beyond our means—"hidden with Christ in God"?

Again it is lives, not gifts, that are in the balance here. The widow is meant to provide a contrast to the scribes (vv. 38–41) with their love of prominence. They hardly thought about life and faith as matters beyond their means. They went about in long robes, marks of professional status. They reveled in salutations in the marketplace. We get the picture of a kind of lusting for titles and rank that will lift one above the crowd, above a colleague: manager, executive, director, doctor. They sought, and then came to expect, the best seats and preferential treatment at public gatherings and private parties. It is not difficult to fill places of honor; someone is always on the make for them.

Just ask James and John. The widow is a contrast to them, too, and also to the other disciples who got into that argument about who was the greatest. "Are you able," said Jesus, "to drink the cup with me . . . ?" "We are able, Lord" (Mark 10:38f.). There was apparently no sense among the Twelve of being beyond their means in meeting the demands of life and faith and the cost of discipleship. But it was from that circle of the Twelve that there came betrayal and denial; and in the end they all "forsook him and fled."

This widow stands over against the multitude putting money in the treasury, among whom were rich folk who put in large sums. Notice that there is no denunciation of the gifts that were given. There is no indication in the text that the rich were anything but generous. In fact, Mark underscores their generosity. Nor is there any indication that they made a big show of their gifts. Jesus simply says that true giving is to be measured not absolutely, by the size of the gift, but proportionately and relative to what is left. The widow's gift was two small coins, the smallest in circulation; but in the eyes of God who looks upon the heart, this was big business. There were two coins: one she could have given and the other she could have kept—a fifty-fifty ratio of benevolences to current expenses, a lofty goal for any individual or congregation.

But no. "Love is a spendthrift," Mark seems to be saying. "Love leaves its arithmetic at home. Love is always 'in the red'" (Paul Scherer). "Truly, I tell you, this poor widow has put in more than all those who are contributing to the treasury. For they all contributed out of their abundance; but she out of her poverty has put in everything she had, her whole living" (Mark 12:43–44).

Even as Jesus utters these final words, a shadow falls across the scene. It is the shadow of a cross. In this poor widow's un-self-conscious act of devotion, Mark points us forward to that cross upon which another placed everything—his whole living.

Here one becomes strikingly aware of the theme of the Epistle lesson (Heb. 9:24–28), and indeed of the emphasis in the whole of the Epistle to the Hebrews on the transcendent order and reality that is mirrored in Jesus Christ. The lesson underscores the sacrifice of Christ as "once-for-all"; one might even say the gift in light of which all other gifts—all acts of stewardship, both of the wealthy and the poor—make sense. Read, for example, Mark 12:41 and Heb. 9:26b in juxtaposition. Does the story of the poor widow not point us toward the greater mystery of the God who holds nothing back in his love for his children?

Perhaps Mark's scene of the poor widow at the temple treasury is a good one to keep before us on the twenty-fifth Sunday after Pentecost as we ponder the issues of stewardship and Thanksgiving. The poignant drama of the widow's offering reminds us that "Love is a spendthrift. Love leaves its arithmetic at home. Love is always 'in the red.'"

In any serious consideration of stewardship and Thanksgiving, therefore, we must go beyond percentages, bottom lines, and net incomes versus gross incomes versus adjusted gross incomes, to the heart of the matter of faith and ownership and gratitude. As that cruciform shadow falls upon the poor widow placing her whole living at the service of God, we can almost hear the music and feel the words begin to form on our lips:

Were the whole realm of nature mine,
That were a present far too small,
Love so amazing, so divine,
Demands my soul, my life, my all.
(Isaac Watts, "When I Survey the Wondrous Cross")

The Twenty-sixth Sunday After Pentecost

Lutheran	Roman Catholic	Episcopal	Pres/UCC/Chr	Meth/COCU
Dan. 12:1–3	Dan. 12:1–3	Dan. 12:1–4a (5–13)	Dan. 12:1–4	Dan. 12:1–13
Heb. 10:11–18	Heb. 10:11–14, 18	Heb. 10:31–39	Heb. 10:11–18	Heb. 10:11–18
Mark 13:1–13	Mark 13:24–32	Mark 13:14–23	Mark 13:24–32	Mark 13:1–13

By the twenty-sixth Sunday after Pentecost, we begin to be aware of things coming to an end. On this last or next-to-last Sunday before Advent, we are at the end of the Christian year. In some regions another harvest is gathered, and many of us will celebrate the national holiday of Thanksgiving by looking back over the year with gratitude and perhaps also with some regret. In any case, among the appointed texts for the end of the Christian year are these strange and difficult ones from Daniel and Mark that speak of the end of all years.

In dramatic symbols and vivid language, these lessons lay claim to the future in the name of One from whom all life and time come forth, and unto whom all life and time are destined to return. They serve to remind us, as seasons come and go in life and in worship, that time itself and our time being, despite all appearances to the contrary, move purposefully forward under the promise and in the providence of God. Notwithstanding the sense of crisis and urgency that beats like a pulse in Mark's thirteenth chapter—Take heed! Wait! Watch! Pray! Get ready!—there is the unmistakable sense of an eternal order and purpose: "Heaven and earth will pass away, but my words will not pass away" (Mark 13:31). There is a certain assurance that when all is said and done, "the Lord God Omnipotent reigneth!" even "though the earth should change, though the mountains shake in the heart of the sea" (Rev. 19:6; Ps. 46:2–3).

To be sure, the note of comfort and security sounded in this strange word about the end of time is sounded against and over the clamor of the false securities, the follies, and the foibles of human existence. One thinks, for example, of human pride in the skill of our hands that seeks security in its own achievements: "Look, Teacher . . . what wonderful buildings!" (Mark 13:1). Jesus worshiped in the temple gladly. But he also knew the danger in all human accomplishments. Great buildings, whether temples or cathedrals, banks or mansions, corporate headquarters or state capitols, cater to human pride and invite a false sense of permanence. "There will not be left . . . one stone upon another . . ." (Mark 13:2). If, for effect, Jesus used an overdrawn metaphor with the disciples, today that word leaps across the centuries, a chilling prophecy in an atomic age: "Not one stone left upon another."

Atomic research has made possible now the suicide or abortion of the human race—capital punishment on a global scale. "Not one stone left upon another" can hardly be dismissed as outmoded biblical language, not when it is in the realm of possibility to turn a small country into a "parking lot," as was suggested by some trigger-happy soul in the heat of the Iranian hostage affair. Common sense and intelligent reflection teach us that the world is hastening toward crisis and disaster. In science and technology, through military alliances and atomic might, we have sought and been promised deliverance from danger and security in our time. However, one reliance after another has failed us. The superpowers continue to out-tough one another in rhetoric and rockets, and insecurity intensifies worldwide under the shadow of our own twentieth-century apocalyptic scenario. Is there any wonder that the stupor or euphoria of drugs and alcohol, the momentary thrill of casual sex, the promised security in the mind control of religious cults are so appealing to so many? We may be today closer than ever to the point of understanding that in the dictionary of human existence, the first word is "dependence" and the last word is "reverence," and both point us to the same Mystery in which life is held—the Lord God who made us for himself, in whose grace and providence alone our security rests, and who, when all is said and done, is the only ultimate hope in life, death, and destiny.

Then there is the folly of our wanting the schedule and the blueprint for the mysterious purposes of this God. "Tell us," said Peter and Andrew and James and John, "when will this be, and what will be the sign when these things are all to be accomplished?" (Mark 13:4). One thing is crucial if we are to understand, and not misunderstand, the Word of God in apocalyptic literature such as we are faced with today in Daniel and Mark. The conviction upon which this literature rests and the message it would proclaim is that the Lord God Omnipotent reigneth—sovereign, gracious, invincible! God's rule is not subject to any other power in heaven or earth. God rules and will rule in the freedom of his invincible grace. Therefore, God will not be tied to any human schedule, nor does his kingdom conform to any human blueprint.

Jesus makes this clear. "No one has the schedule," he says in effect: "But of that day or that hour no one knows, not even the angels in heaven, nor the Son, but only the Father" (Mark 13:32; cf. Acts 1:7). Furthermore, "Take heed that no one lead you astray. Many will come in my name, saying 'I am he!' and they will lead many astray" (Mark 13:5–6). His answer suggests quite clearly the mischief that comes of a blueprint or schedule of God's way in human hands—the harm that can come to life when one is too intent on pinning God down to a date or a scenario, a program or a method. Beware of those who promise, "This is it! Here it is!" expecting us to trade our trust in the promise and the dependability of God's grace for that instant security.

The warnings here are not ancient history. Many a movement, feeding on the ego of its leader, the painful hunger of the people, and the mass hysteria of an uncertain time, has tried to co-opt the Christian name: Reverend Moon (who reports a dream in which Jesus Christ bowed down to him), a whole gaggle of TV "reverends" (safely isolated from human suffering, by the way, in their snug studios)—those people who, as G.K. Chesterton once observed, claim to know the "last word" about everything, but who know the first word about nothing.

Jesus' words, "lead . . . astray" are especially sharp. That is what preoccupation with the end of the world actually does. It leads one astray from the present task of obedience and compassion and trust. To clamor, when? may well be a silly dodge to put off what needs doing now. If all the attention and concern which in Christian history have been given to last things had only been given to first things (cf. Mark 12:29ff.; Matt. 6:33; 25:35ff.), the power of Christian faith in the world, its impact on the world, and its service to the world would have been enormously increased.

The only time there is, is God's time. To God belongs the past which he gathers up in mercy and redeems. To God belongs the future and the triumph of his gracious purposes. To God belongs the present in which, in Jesus Christ and by the power of his Holy Spirit, he elects to be God with us and God for us. In the *Book of Common Prayer* is a collect that helps to put our time being in proper perspective: "Eternal God, who committest to us the swift and solemn trust of life; since we do not know what a day may bring forth, but only that the hour for serving thee is always present, may we wake to the instant claims of thy holy will, not waiting for tomorrow, but yielding today."

So the summons sounds, not to hysteria (the sky is falling!), not to inordinate curiosity (when will the last day be, and what will it be like?) but to fidelity to the Lord Christ, and with it the call to sing out the confident refrain: "The Lord reigns; let the earth rejoice!"

"But take heed to yourselves . . . " (Mark 13:9). Again, Jesus cautions the disciples. This time it is more than a warning; it is more like a promise that the way of Christ will not be easy but a test of endurance and danger. Most of us have to wonder about that, don't we? Our faith has not really put us in any danger, has it? Of course, that might say more about the kind of comfortable Christians we are than it does about either faith or the world. For while the gospel most surely comforts the afflicted, there is also a relentless bias for justice in it that has a way of afflicting the comfortable. Privilege is ill at ease in its presence. Power is suspicious of it, especially when it is discovered that this gospel cannot be seduced, bought off, or co-opted to serve the status quo or the ideology of some revolutionary movement or another. Recall how Jesus affected the Sanhedrin, Pilate, Herod. The Zealots (the revolutionaries) could not cope with his patience, his gentleness, his compassion, his refusal to write off their enemies. And yet Rome (the status quo) outlawed the Christian movement as treason.

From the human standpoint, at least, there is a sense in which the gospel is always on shaky ground. Understood at its depths, it is really not a very good faith for people who think the most important thing in life is winning and being "number one." This is why Christian faith is often so sincerely and yet so incredibly misunderstood by those of us whose approach to life is only that of an athlete, a beauty pageant contestant, a general, or a politician. While all the metaphors may be useful, Christian life is not finally a game, a contest, a battle, a race with success or even with salvation as the prize. Christian faith is a gift that calls us to a task.

At times there is little the Christian can do except pray, take the lumps, and wait. Sometimes one has, in the words of Robert Louis Stevenson, only "the half of broken hope for a pillow," only the "shade of a word" for comfort. At times the kingdom lags and the promises of God are discounted as "too slow" in meeting the problems of the world. And here the church must not become overly defensive; we must confess our failures. Too often we are unprofitable servants. Nevertheless, times and seasons are *subjects,* not sovereign, in a kingdom that is "from everlasting to everlasting."

We must not, however, be glib about this business of human suffering. For all the joy, security, and fulfillment we can point to and give thanks for, there is sorrow, fear, and despair aplenty. There is thick darkness of suffering and tragedy: a husband lying there dying, or a daughter who perhaps would be better off so; children needing food and warm clothing now with winter coming on, and a job gone with the latest layoff, and the tender ties of home and family rubbed raw by the mounting stress and fear as the end of the month closes in with more payments due on top of last month's unpaid bills. "The evil of life," wrote Abbe' Ernest Dimnet, "is felt in its full force by people who simply shake their heads and never say a word."[11]

God pity us if all we can offer for human woe is some glib commonplace: "Be of good cheer!" "Keep your chin up!" "Have a nice day!" The Stoics used to manage that. For the Christian, the answer is not a creed or a philosophy of life. It is God—the I and Thou of God—not standing by looking on idly, doing nothing, but throwing himself into the fray, until from the sovereignty of his grace and love there comes the overpowering of evil by goodness, the undoing of sin by mercy; and out of darkness, light; and out of pain, healing; and out of death, life. That is the stuff by which Christian faith lives.

That is why Mark put this so-called little apocalypse here between the end of Jesus' public ministry in chapter 12 and his Passion and resurrection. By this arrangement Mark says that the God to whom the future belongs is One who in Jesus Christ, out of sheer grace and in steadfast love, suffers and dies with us and for us and is raised to rule as Lord of life. He it is who claims the future and our future as his possession and not evil, sin, destruction, and death. Out of that comes the summons to fidelity, to confidence, and to reverent obedience. Thus we see the supreme importance of Jesus' words: "Take heed to yourselves."

He might well have added: "And trust in the triumph of God." Read again Mark 13:24–26. The literal picture and imagery here are only husk, not the kernel of truth. The good news is something deeper: the faith that God is the Factor in the world yesterday, today, forever; that he will redeem human history; that every person's life adds up to something that is already envisioned in the mind and heart and intention of God; that the conquest of evil and sin and death comes not out of our wit and muscle, but by the grace of God—free, sovereign, invincible. Is that the distant music of hope?

There is a total purposefulness about life, all its varied notes fitting somehow into a sort of stirring symphony. That confession is flung down here by Mark as a kind of "nevertheless" of faith. In the face of what Keats called the "giant agony of the world," and without for a moment denying the darkness and the pain, Mark stands Jesus Christ at the center of things—even suggests that we read the future and the finale of life through his cross and resurrection—as if to say: "Here is where you go for the conviction of God's overruling providence!"

When all is said and done, who knows what will happen? What we do know, wrote Frederick Beuchner, is that "in a world without God we know at least that the thing that will happen will be a human thing, a thing no better or no worse than the most that humanity itself can be. But in a world with God, we can never know what will happen. . . . "[12] God might even come to us in person. God might even take our humanity in all its wholeness and brokenness upon himself, to himself. God might even laugh with us, cry with us, strive with us, and suffer with us. God might even die with us, go with us to death and through death. God might even show us, in person, that sin is overcome by forgiveness, that evil is undone by goodness, that death is swallowed up in the victory of his invincible grace.

In the meantime, the world we live in needs the ministry of the church—the worship of God, the teaching of the faith, the fellowship, the mutual service, the social witness in deeds of compassion and in acts of kindness and tenderness and justice. On this Sunday at or near the end of the Christian year, the lessons invite us, nay, summon us, to recommit ourselves to that—to the celebration and proclamation and fleshing out of the good news that God is sovereign in the earth, that Jesus Christ is

Lord of life and of death, and that when all is said and done Exodus and
Easter, not bondage and death, are the determinative events that claim
the future.

Compare the Epistle lesson in Heb. 10:11–18 with its picture of Christ
seated at the right hand of God, having completed for all time the new
covenant of grace for forgiveness, reconciliation, and redemption. This
lesson gathers up the meaning of Dan. 12:1–4 and Mark 13 and points
forward to the lessons and the theme of the twenty-seventh Sunday in
Pentecost—Christ the King. This we shall deal with at length in the final
chapter. However, if the year does not afford us a twenty-seventh Sunday in Pentecost, this Epistle text at least sounds a fanfare and points us
to the crucified Lord: risen, ascended, reigning.

Christ the King
The Last Sunday After Pentecost

Lutheran	Roman Catholic	Episcopal	Pres/UCC/Chr	Meth/COCU
Dan. 7:13–14	Dan. 7:13–14	Dan. 7:9–14	Dan. 7:13–14	Dan. 7:13–14
Rev. 1:4b–8	Rev. 1:5–8	Rev. 1:1–8	Rev. 1:4–8	Rev. 1:1–8
John 18:33–37	John 18:33–37	John 18:33–37 or Mark 11:1–11	John 18:33–37	John 18:33–37

"Grace to you and peace . . . from Jesus Christ . . . the ruler of kings
on earth" (Rev. 1:4–5). Thus John greets the churches to whom he
addresses the Book of the Revelation with its great vision of the con-
summation of history. The lectionary pairs this Epistle text, Rev. 1:4b–8,
with the "night vision" in Dan. 7:13–14 for the final Sunday of the
Christian year, Christ the King. It is a concluding testimony to the
significance of Jesus Christ for us and for our world before we embark
once again on the Advent journey to Bethlehem.

By so designating this final Sunday, the liturgy of the church underscores the convergence, the intersecting, of kingdoms. The issue is

joined dramatically in this scene of Jesus before Pilate. Some thirty years before, a decree had gone out from Caesar Augustus and brought a Jewish couple from Nazareth to Bethlehem, in a far corner of the Roman Empire, where the woman had given birth to a child and laid him in a manger. That birth, according to tradition, had drawn "kings" from the East to worship, they said, the newborn "king of the Jews," which raised the suspicion of one Herod the Great who assumed he was king of the Jews.

It is as if there is some implication in all this for the kingdoms of this world. The whole issue is played out here, some thirty years later, as Christ stands before Pilate and says: "My kingdom is not of this world . . . For this I was born and for this I have come into the world, to bear witness to the truth" (John 18:36, 37). The drama is so poignant that one almost has to wonder if it really could have happened in so perfect a way. There is Pontius Pilate representing the kingdom of this world. The kingdom in particular that Pilate represented, the Roman Empire, was synonymous with ruthless power and rule by intimidation. Rome had the organization, the personnel, the power of arms, and the willingness to use them in the interest of her empire. The cross that looms over this scene of Jesus before Pilate was just one of many, remember. Tens of thousands had died by crucifixion before Jesus ever graced that scaffold. Every schoolchild knew what it was to walk out of the house and see the gaunt form of a cross standing out against the sky beside the road and to shudder at the sight: the rule of intimidation.

So there is Pilate, and there is Jesus representing another kingdom, a kingdom *not* of this world. The paradox is that while Jesus is powerless before Pilate, he is majestic beyond Pilate's comprehension. Pilate views Jesus as people of power always view pure goodness, namely, with a mixture of admiration, contempt, and an uneasiness that borders on fear. It is there in Pilate's question: "Are you the king of the Jews?" Pilate's concern was not a religious concern. It was as political as it could be: how much of a threat to his power, to the kingdom of this world, would this man Jesus represent? "Are you just a harmless dreamer?" Pilate wanted to know, "or are you a threat to the social order?" "Art thou king of the Jews?" It is the question that centers of power, be they individual or national, always seem to ask when confronted by the kingdom not of this world: enemy or friend? Art thou king?

Only the answer Jesus gave is not quite so easy for us to fathom. Said he: "My kingdom is not of this world. . . ." Now Pilate hoped Jesus meant that he was not concerned with this life, only with the life to come. After all, if Christ and his church are not really interested in questions of justice, or concerned with how people are treated and mistreated, then the kings and kingdoms of this world really have nothing ultimately to fear. If Pilate can be assured that Christ's kingdom is not of this world and without serious concern for this world, then the status quo is not threatened, and the rule of intimidation goes on unchallenged. Perhaps too we shall hear a misunderstanding Pilate say to us what he said to the religious and political leaders of his own day: "I find no fault at all in the man."

But what if Jesus' answer is simpler, more straightforward, and also more profound than we usually suppose? That is to say, in the midst of the kingdoms of this world, there is a kingdom of justice, truth, goodness, and peace that stands over against them in judgment and redemption. To the rule of intimidation, to the politics of dishonesty and deceit and expediency, there really is an alternative, namely, a rule of grace and truth. This kingdom, this rule, is the kingdom of God and his righteousness. In the deepest sense, it is not *of* this world, but it is very definitely at work *in* this world and is sharply focused in the person of Jesus of Nazareth. The Gospel lessons all through Pentecost, especially those from Mark, have focused on Jesus as the one in whom God's sovereign rule of grace, the kingdom of God, has come near.

The sovereignty of God is the grand premise in the Bible. We meet it on page one: "In the beginning, God created the heavens and the earth . . ." (Gen. 1:1). It runs through the whole from Genesis to Revelation. But God's sovereignty is an odd sort of sovereignty. There is no doubt about God's being in control, but God is not pictured as a ruthless tyrant, ruling by coercive force, demanding rigid, reflex compliance. God's sovereignty expresses itself in his far-reaching expectations for his human family, and for their life together—life from God, through God, and to God. This is the substance and purpose of the Law, the Torah. But God's sovereignty makes room in creation for the mysteries of human personality and human freedom.

It is a strange sort of sovereignty. The people of Israel struggle with it; Jonah runs away from it; Job argues with it. Over and again, stories of disobedience and incidents of rebellion in the lives of heroes like Moses,

David, and Joseph and in the history of the nation testify that the sovereignty of God is not irresistible. It is resisted all the time! But what means more for the triumph of righteousness is that, however resistible it might be, God's sovereignty is, nonetheless, invincible. Men and women can do things that will diminish their humanity; they *cannot* do things that can dethrone God or nullify his purposes for them.

This sovereignty of God is God's righteous rule in the world and in human affairs; and it is rule in the dynamic, active sense: it orders, guides, directs, sets limits, blocks off excesses in worship and in human behavior. But it is not enforced by coercion or intimidation. Failure to live under the sovereignty of God, living as if there were no God, results not in naked retaliation; it generates its own retribution; it is *self-defeating*. Even when the Bible speaks of the wrath or judgment of God, it does not picture God concerned with getting even or exacting his pound of flesh in punishment for his wounded pride.

The wrath of God is God's refusal to indulge men and women in their disobedience and folly. It is God's letting us do what we want to do, but refusing to be party to it. What greater downfall could a person have than to reach the end of his or her career, having clawed and scraped one's way to the top, without God? This would be the downfall of all downfalls: to perceive at the end of my life that I had done what I wanted to do and become what I wanted to be, that my planning had succeeded and my goal had been reached, *without God.* So God refuses to go along with his people in their pride and folly; still, he never gives them up. To bear with us may well break God's heart, but the one thing this sovereign God cannot bear, it seems, is to give us up. So the judgment of God is very real, but it is never mere vengeance, never an end in itself. It is, rather, a means to reconciliation and atonement.

Here is where we come on the theme of God's steadfast love, his unmerited mercy, his grace. "The Lord is gracious and merciful, slow to anger and abounding in steadfast love . . ." (Ps. 103:8). There is a sense of God's sovereignty as flexible, patient, "laid back." He is more concerned with the well-being of his people than with their swift and unquestioning submission. From the standpoint of the Bible, the doctrine of perseverance applies more to God than to the saints. God's sovereignty, as the rule of grace, is surely a sovereignty not of *this* world.

Thus, when Jesus came preaching the kingdom of God and his righteousness, he was misunderstood at almost every turn. The revolutionaries thought the kingdom meant a new pecking order under which they would benefit. The disciples argued about status and rank and who was to sit where at the banquet table of the kingdom. The scribes and Pharisees thought God's righteousness would confirm them in their righteousness, which led them into *self*-righteousness. The powerful, like Herod and Pilate, were yet so insecure that in any mention of another kingdom, they heard only "sedition" and "treachery," trembled in their boots, and lashed out in fear.

Therefore, Jesus turned to parables to show what on earth he meant by the kingdom of God—the kingdom not of this world—that was nevertheless "at hand." The parables, however, do not solve the mystery; they highlight it. They do not define the kingdom of God; they point to it. They do not tell us what it is, only what it is *like*. They give glimpses of insight into God's kingdom, not blueprints or charters or constitutions; and thus they were and still are a bafflement to the hardnosed, the tidy-minded, and the literalists.

Furthermore, these parables are very disconcerting to the powerful. They tell of an enterprise—the kingdom of God—that is not finally dependent on what men and women do or decide one way or another. They describe an order of life and human relationships based not on a chain of command, but on compassion and mutuality; marked not by strict proportion, but by appropriate caring; concerned not with what is lawful according to the dictates of the big shots in church or state or community, but with what is right and fitting. The parables point to an order of reality that depends finally not on diligence, but on providence.

Look at how these parables stack the kingdom of God and his righteousness up against the kingdoms of this world. Take the parable of the laborers in the vineyard (Matt. 20:1-16): in the kingdom of this world, one gets what one deserves, either positively or negatively, reward or punishment, quid pro quo. In the kingdom of God, what rules is grace, not merit, the extravagance of God's love, not the bottom line of a wage and hour schedule.

The parable of the lost sheep and the good shepherd who leaves the ninety-nine and seeks the one who is lost (Luke 15:1-7) reminds us that in the kingdom of God there is no cost benefit accounting—that grace asks what is fitting and appropriate, not what is efficient. The parable of the good Samaritan (Luke 10:25–37) sets the Samaritan over against the busy priest and Levite and says that under the rule of grace there is time for doing all the good one can. The parable of the prodigal son and the elder brother (Luke 15:11–32) is a perfect parable of grace: in the kingdom of God love is not based on merit, but is full of mercy; it is not evenhanded, but appropriate and fitting whatever the circumstances; it is not conditional, but "out of all *due* proportion." The parable of the wheat and tares growing together (Matt. 13:24–30) says that in the kingdom of God patience is more important than efficiency, and that the patience of God in allowing the tares to grow along with the wheat until the harvest gives us all a better future than we deserve.

This is the kingdom that is "at hand." It is not ours for the having, the claiming, the possessing, the manipulating for our own advantage and interest. It is, however, ours for the *receiving*—a very subtle and profound distinction that goes to the roots of faith and trust.

"My kingdom is not of this world," said Jesus. "For this I was born and for this I have come into the world, to bear witness to the truth. Everyone who is of the truth hears my voice." To this Pilate sneered the sneer that always comes from people of power in the world when the kingdom not of this world stakes its claim. "Truth?" said Pilate, "What's that?"

Now John's Gospel, all the way through, makes a great deal of truth and light as two ways of understanding the meaning of Jesus Christ for us today. It does not regard truth as a theorem, but as an event, a revelatory event, that gives meaning to all other events in the world, shining a light on them in order that we may see them as they really are. Jesus, says John, is that event: "I was born for this," says Jesus, "to bear witness to the truth" (John 18:37). And with his birth, in relation to which now both atheist and believer alike date their daily mail, we are given to see the kingdom not of this world breaking in upon us in judgment and in hope.

Once in a public park, the story is told, a spectator at a chess game was overheard to say of a certain move on the chess board: "That's it!" By that he meant that although the other contestant might squirm for a time and even for a long time prolong the game, that one decisive move had determined the outcome of the whole game. The opponent might not yet believe it; the other spectators might not have noticed; but that one spectator knew, and because he knew, he watched the rest of the game in a different light. In the liturgy of the church, the final Sunday of the year, Christ the King, plays the role of that one perceptive man. In faith—faith being our response to the beckoning of the mystery and to the claim laid upon us by the kingdom not of this world—in faith, the Bible tells the story of Christ before Pilate and says: "That's it!" God has made his move in human story, and that gives meaning to every other move in all the world. It shines a revealing light on all other events so that now at least we can see things as they really are.

"For this I was born and for this I have come into the world, to bear witness to the truth. Everyone who is of the truth hears my voice." This is what is at stake in the encounter between Jesus and Pilate. The kingdom of God confronts the kingdom of this world. The rule of grace confronts the rule of intimidation, and in that confrontation ultimate questions arise, causing people like us to wonder what is up in our world and to whom the future belongs.

"My kingdom is not of this world." In no way do those words mean that the Christian is to take a hands-off attitude toward the world. Jesus Christ is God's laying hold of the whole world—the kingdom of this world staking its claim upon this world and those who dwell therein.

"My kingdom is not of this world." Neither does that mean that the Christian's life in the world is an ungoverned life, a life without standards. Christian life is life under the rule of grace, under the standard, the banner, of the kingdom of God and his righteousness. It reflects the truth and light of its Lord. It is *patient,* reflecting God's long suffering. God's patience, remember, is not softheartedness; it is not God's unwillingness to take hold of a situation. Patience, rather, derives from God's own largeheartedness, the heart of God that is "big as all outdoors." Christian life means *faithfulness*—a steadiness in life reflecting God's own steadfastness that holds on to us even when we are hardly worth the holding. Faithfulness means living with confidence in God's grace and without dread that God is tricking us or that his grace will not last. Christian life is marked by *gentleness* (the King James Version frequently translates it "meekness") and *modesty.* Gentleness means not flaunting oneself, not calling attention to oneself, a sort of un-self-conscious graciousness. It means not throwing one's weight around or using one's position or power to mistreat or oppress another person, not spiking the football when one makes a touchdown. We could go on to other marks of grace in life: compassion, generosity, self-control; we begin to get the picture.

To live under grace does not mean to have miraculous powers or special protection from trouble. It does mean to have a more open and thankful heart, and in the words of the Heidelberg Catechism, "to be patient in adversity, grateful in the midst of blessing, and to trust our faithful God and Father for the future, assured that no creature shall separate us from his love, since all creatures are so completely in his hand that without his will they cannot even move."

Still, it is not easy, not painless, not without struggle and striving and suffering. It never was, never is, never will be. Even as Jesus stands before Pilate, the shadow of a cross falls on the scene. Said Pilate and the chief priests and the Roman soldiers and the crowd and the disciples: "So much for the kingdom not of this world." But they, none of them, reckoned with that strange sovereignty of God who can let himself be nailed to a scaffold and sealed in a tomb and still not be done for. None of them reckoned with that grace which, while it may be irresistible, is nonetheless invincible.

In this season of Thanksgiving, here at the end of the Christian year, before we begin another Advent pilgrimage to Bethlehem, receive this greeting: "Grace to you and peace . . . from Jesus Christ . . . ruler of kings on earth." Could that be the music to which you and I are expected to walk upon our several ways and across the days and years of our lives and our life together? "Grace to you and peace . . . from Jesus Christ . . . ruler of kings on earth." As it opens into life, that music has a way of becoming a symphony or a great chorus. At least George Frederick Handel found it so. Remember how he gathered up this theme? "The kingdom of this world has become the kingdom of our Lord and of his Christ; and he shall reign forever and ever. King of Kings, and Lord of Lords. Hallelujah!"[13]

Notes

1. Cf. André Bieler, *The Social Humanism of Calvin,* trans. Paul T. Fuhrmann (Richmond: John Knox Press, 1964), 27–42.
2. Karl Barth, *The Great Promise,* trans. Hans Freund (New York: Philosophical Library, 1963), 53.
3. Cf. Karl Barth, *Church Dogmatics,* 4 vols., ed. G. W. Bromiley and T. F. Torrance, trans. G. W. Bromiley et al. (Edinburgh: T. & T. Clark, 1957), 2.2:617–18.
4. Reinhold Niebuhr, *The Irony of American History* (New York: Charles Scribner's Sons, 1952), 63.
5. H. Richard Niebuhr, *The Meaning of Revelation* (New York: Macmillan Co., 1941), 36.
6. Ibid., 93.
7. Ibid., 93, 152.
8. Note how, along with the voice from heaven in the story of the transfiguration (9:7) and the discussion about the power of Jesus' name in overcoming the demons (9:38ff.), this healing of Bartimaeus's blindness serves to underscore Jesus' authority as he speaks about servanthood and the cost of discipleship.
9. Augustine, *Serm. (de Script. Nov. Test.)* 141.4.4. See also Erick Przywara, *An Augustine Synthesis* (Magnolia, Mass.: Peter Smith Publisher, n.d.), 198. The quotation concludes H. Richard Niebuhr's *The Meaning of Revelation,* 191. I am indebted to Robert McAfee Brown, *The Spirit of Protestantism* (New York and London: Oxford University Press, 1965), 235 for the documentation cited above.
10. Peter Taylor Forsyth, *The Principle of Authority* (London: Independent Press, 1952), 342.
11. Cited by Paul Scherer, *The Interpreter's Bible,* 12 vols., ed. George A. Buttrick (Nashville: Abingdon Press, 1951), 8:366.
12. Frederick Buechner, *The Hungering Dark* (New York: Seabury Press, 1969), 123.
13. George F. Handel, *Messiah,* cf. Rev. 19:16; 11:15.